IN THIS BOOK:

1. Ancient knowledge of secret power for directing your own destiny.

2. How to live, apply and consciously experience the hidden cosmic forces represented by the Qabala Tree of Life.

INNER FREEDOM THROUGH QABALA

by BOB LANCER

Limitless Light Publishing

ISBN: 0-917913-02-7

Printed in the United States of America

Cover Art by Edwin B. Hirth III

Published by:
    LIMITLESS LIGHT PUBLISHING
    8115-1 N. 35th Ave.
    Phoenix, Arizona 85051

DEDICATION

This book is lovingly dedicated to my precious wife, Aviva. Without her tireless work and dedication it would not have been.

ACKNOWLEDGEMENTS

The help and work of many and those who went before contribute indispensably to any final product. The author here wishes to gratefully acknowledge the efforts of the following groups and individuals who have directly and indirectly been of help:

ISIDORE FRIEDMAN

The **NATURAL ORDER WISDOM CENTER**
And specifically its members:
Ed Parker
Christine Parker
Kandi Paris
Dennis Reuter

The **SCHOOL OF THE NATURAL ORDER**
Founded by Vitvan
Which continues to make Vitvan's
Esoteric Wisdom Teachings available.
For further information write:
The School Of The Natural Order
P.O. Box 578
Baker, Nevada 89311

The **INSTITUTE OF GENERAL SEMANTICS**
Founded by Alfred Korzybski
Which continues to distribute Alfred Korzybski's
monumental work of insight:
SCIENCE AND SANITY

INNER FREEDOM THROUGH QABALA

by Bob Lancer

TABLE OF CONTENTS

Introduction viii

Part I: Journey Through the Spheres 11

Sphere 1: The Crown 12

Sphere 2: Wisdom 22

Sphere 3: Understanding 30

Sphere 4: Mercy 38

Sphere 5: Severity 46

Sphere 6: Beauty 54

Sphere 7: Victory 62

Sphere 8: Glory 70

Sphere 9: Foundation 78

Sphere 10: The Kingdom 86

Part II: Applications of the System as a Whole 97

Inner Freedom Through Qabala 98

The Qabalist's Formula for Fulfillment 108

Meditating With Qabala 118

Poem: Qabala Meditation 129

Illustration: Qabala Tree of Life 13

"The first purpose of life is to discover the purpose of life."

Ancient Qabalistic Axiom

INTRODUCTION

It is likely that you who are reading this have a question in mind. What is "Qabala" (pronounced: Kabalah)? Relatively few ever heard the word, although the number of those who have heard it is growing.

Qabala is a Hebrew word meaning "From mouth to ear" or "Oral Teaching". Just what is meant by the phrase "Oral Teaching" has been and can be interpreted any number of ways, according to one's background.

For the purposes of this present volume, we can say that Qabala is the name of a powerful and subtle Wisdom Teaching that has been handed down from Enlightened Teacher to Aspiring Student through age after age. As a Wisdom Teaching, its aim is the upliftment of the human being, that we might discover our own True Divine Nature, express it naturally, and thereby assume our rightful place in the Cosmic Process.

Throughout the ages there have been Wisdom Teachers and Wisdom Teachings, though extremely few genuine articles existing at any one time. These Teachings have taken on many forms and names. What stands Qabala apart is that it centers itself around a simple yet subtly compelling diagram called **THE TREE OF LIFE.** (pictured on page 13).

This diagram and the Wisdom it represents is the focus of this book. The explanation and application of it to our daily living for fulfilling the High Cosmic Purpose of our lives begins in the first chapter. For now, let it suffice to say that fulfilling that Purpose is the only true and lasting source of happiness, and failing to do so the only cause of suffering.

Upon hearing of Qabala individuals tend to ask: "Where does it come from?" and "Why is it named in Hebrew?" The answer to the first question is not possible.

Its origin is uncertain as far as any of the ordinary, tangible, historical evidence is able to tell us. But there are legends, one of which may contain far more truth and validity than we "modern, mature adults" may assume. This legend asserts that Qabala, and the Tree of Life on which it is based, was given to man by the Angels. The purpose of this gift was to give man a Key to the mysteries of the universe and the process of his return to his own Divine Origin which is WITHIN. What we do know of Qabala's history is that it has been known about by a few, and Understood and applied by far fewer, for a long, long time.

This Wisdom Teaching, which we can accurately describe as *esoteric* (meaning known only by the few), was presented and discussed in the Hebrew language many centuries ago, as written records prove. These can be found in any large public library, although the English spelling of the word Qabala varies, and that might add a degree of difficulty. Since those ancient days, the name for the Teaching which is based on the Tree of Life has stuck, and with it many other Hebrew terms. In this present volume, all but the Teaching's name is presented in English.

Finally, in presenting this book of ancient, though AGELESS, Wisdom, the reader is entitled to ask where the author got his knowledge and information regarding the Qabala. Qabala was introduced to me early in life. It was not too long after I had first heard of it that my life began to take on a radical change for the better (as I perceive it).

Over years of work and study, and with the aid of a private teacher, new levels of consciousness unfolded, and how to APPLY the Wisdom of the Qabala Tree of Life became clear. This present volume is the result of years of work, practical application, and carefully scrutinized experience. Essentially, it is a How To book, almost a kind of Esoteric Wisdom Manual. It is intended for those who want to actually apply and experience their own creative forces, and penetrate into the mysteries of Cosmos and their own True Selves. It is for you who want to solve your daily problems responsibly and effectively, grow and change into a Higher Being, and create with knowledge and blessed power unfathomable.

In closing this introduction, it should be stated that this book merely scratches the surface of the vast storehouse of practical, even *crucial* knowledge which is associated with Qabala. However, there is much to *chew on* here, and a good deal of super techniques for *awakening* us to the limitless light, joy, and peace profound which this universe offers.

May you be blessed by this Teaching and through it, experience that awakening... to your own True Self *within*.

Bob Lancer
6/7/85

PART I

A JOURNEY
THROUGH THE SPHERES

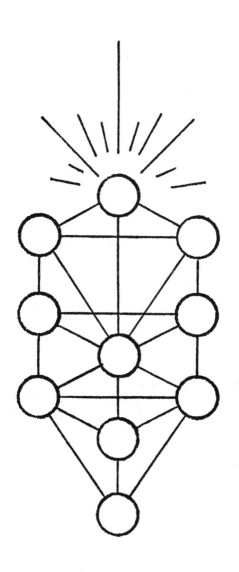

SPHERE 1:
THE CROWN

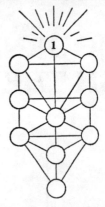

The purpose of studying Qabala is deep. For this is some of what it shows us:

    1) The ten functions of the Enlightened Being

    2) How to find and fulfill your Cosmic Purpose

    3) The ten Cosmic Laws of success, growth, and continuation

    4) How to perceive and live in harmony with the True Nature and Laws of the Cosmic Process

    5) How to discover and consciously identify with your Divine Origin.

All this is involved in that simple diagram called the Qabala Tree of Life, which is pictured on the following page. Each circle on the Tree is called a Sphere, and represents one aspect of the Way of Life of the Enlightened Being. The straight lines which join the Spheres are called Paths. These basically describe the way the Spheres interelate, how they influence one another.

Qabala shows the way to make the present incarnation an expression of your True Self which is within you. This True Self alignment and expression alone, the deeper Wisdom teachings have always held, is the actual way to happiness, Truth Consciousness, and to growth and success in all worthwhile things.

Every Sphere is important. Together, they constitute the ten aspects of One Way. Each represents a way of

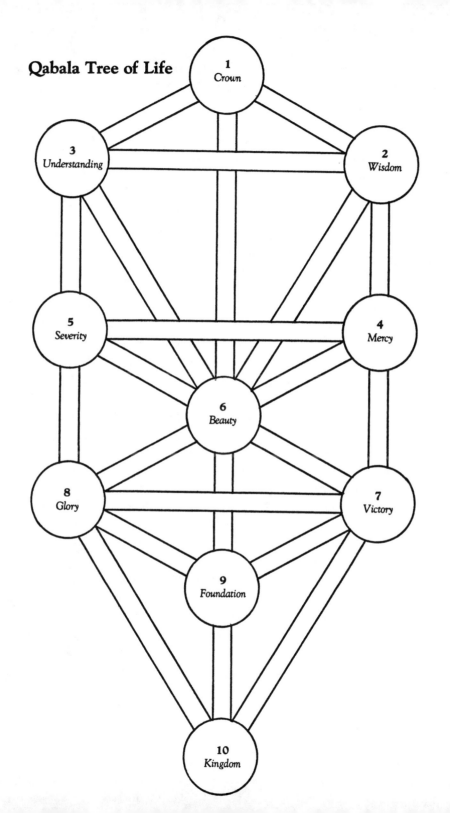

Qabala Tree of Life

living in the now and an objective to fulfill in the future. Living and working consciously on each and all is the **KEY** to a successful business, relationship, Quest for Truth, and **ANY** other endeavor which one might pursue.

Everything stated so far in this volume about Qabala can be **PROVEN** by **YOU**. This book illuminates **HOW** to work on and express each aspect in daily living, and how to apply them to specific needs and goals. Through the application of these methods, one can see the results for himself.

Following is a brief description of the meaning of each Sphere:
Sphere #1: **THE CROWN** - True Perception
Sphere #2: **WISDOM** - conscious control of activity
Sphere #3: **UNDERSTANDING** - insightful awareness into how something works
Sphere #4: **MERCY** - gentleness, leniency, gratification
Sphere #5: **SEVERITY** - discipline, force, focus
Sphere #6: **BEAUTY** - harmony, balance, wholeness, order
Sphere #7: **VICTORY** - fulfillment of desire
Sphere #8: **GLORY** - respected by self and others in the light of Truth
Sphere #9: **FOUNDATION** - strength, stability, endurance
Sphere #10: **THE KINGDOM** - manifestation, completion, earthly or material plane

To leave out **ANY** or all of these ten factors in any project is to guarantee its failure. And as we consciously work on each aspect, we guarantee our success and fulfillment in that area.

Qabala, then, is the way of wholeness, fulfillment, and balanced integration. It integrates or incorporates the Quest for Truth with intelligent action, decency, order, fulfillment, and earthly responsiblilty. Any business, work of art, or individual which does this will know success in its truest, highest, most complete sense. The Qabala Tree of Life shows the way to approach and deal with any and all problems for their adequate solutions; the way to live a healthy, happy, meaningful life.

The first Sphere on the Tree is named The Crown. This represents the highest and most important thing any of us can do. It is the Quest for Truth.

To Quest for Truth means to work at seeing into the True Nature of things, the way things **REALLY** are.

All true Qabalists know this to be an endless process. The more we actually try to see into things, the more we see. It never ends. But it stops when we are not making the effort.

This effort to see into things begins with just trying to sense what is happening more clearly in the now.

Who and what are you really? What are your True needs for a happy life? What is the actual nature of what is going on around you in the here and now? What is the ultimate totality of what you are experiencing in the present? What do you need to do **RIGHT NOW** for the fulfillment of yourself and others in Truth?

Right now, let us make that effort to sense more clearly what is happening, to see what it feels like and what it really means to do it. Take a nice long breath, softly and gently. Relax your body by surveying it for any tensions and releasing them when noticed. Now, try to penetrate the veil of appearances and sense reality.

It is really a matter of paying more attention while realizing there are deeper, truer, brighter levels of awareness of what is happening than we are presently experiencing.

Try, now, to actually sense that, to feel the presence of greater awareness at the threshold of your present state. This helps us become more aware in the present.

When we are actually making this kind of effort, we are making progress. This effort produces the results of clearer conscious awareness of what is happening, who we are dealing with, our own True Selves, etc.

According to Qabala, this needs to be a continuous effort. Are you still trying to be more aware in the now? Some of us **THINK** we do this all the time. We can reason it out that way. We can say, "Well, in a way, isn't everyone doing this all the time?" This kind of thing shows plain and simple confusion and self deceit.

To work on becoming more aware does **NOT** take place unless we are actually observing ourselves making the intentional effort to be so!

Take one day of life and try to remember to make this effort all the time. When we try this we are often surprised to see how much we actually **FORGET** to do it.

Actually trying to be more aware in the now, to pierce the veil of appearances and awaken to the true nature of what is happening, carries us to new levels of conscious perception. We soon begin to sense energies, vibrations, that we used to be unconscious of. We observe moods and attitudes and desires radiating from ourselves and others more clearly. Our mental activities, speech, and actions that used to be UNconscious gradually emerge into the light of our conscious awareness.

Let us try to enter the deeper state of *self-consciousness* now. Try to sense and observe your feelings, the vibrations now happening within you. Become extra observant of any mental activity. Try to stay aware in the now.

Next, become more clearly aware of another in your life or environment. By keeping your consciousness fixed on your own inner vibrations, try to sense and more clearly know that other individual's structure, function, and order. This is not a mental process, but a conscious *feeling* effort to sense that other's basic state in the now.

The effort to stay aware of what is happening in the here-now, of ourselves and of others constitutes the Quest for Truth, work on the Crown Sphere. As we make this effort, we guarantee our continued growth into new levels of awakening.

In time, we see into the level known as Noetic Light. In this level, one is so aware that he consciously registers the vibrations known as Light Frequencies. From awareness of vibrations one becomes clearly conscious in Light's Regions, and identifies consciously with his True Self which lives in Noetic Light, the Light of True Perception. This is a real level, a real experience, that eventually unfolds after years of work and effort on becoming more clearly aware of reality's true nature.

And Noetic Light is considered only the first degree or level of Light's Regions. The ascension into vaster fields of Truth Consciousness is endless. But **WE** must make the continual daily effort.

Working on awareness is the most practical thing we can do. As we try to actually see into the true nature of ourselves, we discover our needs, our abilities, our potentials in ever expanding views. By trying to see into the true nature of others, the same kind of knowledge pertaining to them unfolds. Thus, we can serve ourselves and others better and better.

No business person is really secure until this effort to awaken is carried on. To continually look into the true nature of our business or job, how we are affecting others, what changes or improvements need to be made and what is the best way to go about it, etc. is all vitally important for continued growth and success.

Developing awareness is the key to problem solving. Right now, let us apply it to a problem to see how it works. Bring to your mind a current problem or difficulty that you are facing in your life. When you think of one, try to sense its true nature. Try to see INTO it to sense and feel an awakening to its essential structure, function, order. Try to see more clearly, thoroughly, and deeply into what it is that you are confronted with.

Do you see how it is done? This constitutes the effort to become clearly aware of exactly what it is that is troubling you. With that effort, try to become clearly aware of the True and Essential solution, what you can actually do to SOLVE your problem.

Qabala teaches that it is not enough to simply work on the Crown Sphere, the Quest for Truth, on a sporadic basis. Let us observe ourselves right now, to insure that whatever else we are doing, we are trying to see into the True Nature of where we are, what is happening in the now.

Then, on a regular basis, take time out of your busy day to direct effort into the clear seeing into the true nature of the various areas, responsibilities, and projects of your life. Try to see into the True Nature of how to bring about more harmonious relationships, success in your career, discovery and fulfillment of your True Self, and oneness with the Cosmic Process.

Ultimately, all our needs and goals can be boiled down to just one: *oneness with the Cosmic Process.* Right now, try to sense reality, what is really going on in the now. Feel your awareness linking up with the True Nature in Light's Regions. Begin to try to sense, feel, know, and consciously experience a deeper, fuller sense of being harmoniously integrated with the whole, vast, infinite Cosmic Process in the now.

While walking, washing the dishes, or humming our favorite tunes, we can practice the effort to expand and clarify our awareness into reality. As we do, more awareness unfolds to guide and bring wholeness and harmony to our beings and our lives.

Remember, the effort begins with the acceptance of the fact that there is more to be aware of than we presently are. Then, it proceeds with actually trying to sense more clearly in the now **WHAT IS HAPPENING.**

This effort in itself tends to bring about a balancing, calming sense of peace and harmony. When we are troubled or worrying over something, the effort to see clearly in the now, to more clearly awaken to what is happening or what we can do in the situation confronting us, relieves the suffering and replaces it with cool, calm, healing light.

Making the effort to see and sense and be aware more clearly is a new way to live in the now, and a new way to approach and handle our choices and decisions.

It is the way of the Crown that leads to the Highest High.

SPHERE 2:
WISDOM

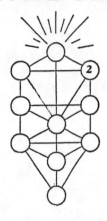

The Qabala Tree of Life provides us with a **TEN PART SYSTEM** leading to growth, achievement, and fulfillment. This is all accomplished through the gradual awakening process to Noetic Light, the Light of True Perception of what **IS,** and **WHAT WE ARE.**

In Noetic Light, we enter conscious identity with our Divine or Higher Self, not as a mere concept or belief, but as **EXPERIENCE.** When you enter a bright room after being in the dark, the light is not a concept or belief. It is an experience. Entering Noetic Light is like that, but it is experienced on a level and to a degree that brings infinitely more *reality* with it. In fact, it brings with it a realization that one is experiencing, really experiencing what **IS,** for the first time.

We have seen just one of the Qabala aspects so far, The Crown, and how it relates to this process of True Awakening and Fulfillment. But the Tree shows us nine other parts. Because ten ways of living and dealing with things are given, all ten are important. For together they provide the way of life for fulfilling our True Purpose.

When we are not applying one of the aspects or Spheres, we are to be applying one of the others. None is to be worked on exclusively. All are to be applied in a whole, balanced, ordered manner. But every moment we are to be working consciously on one of them.

The second Sphere on the Tree is named Wisdom. Wisdom also leads us to Enlightenment; that is, conscious union with our True Self and the True Structure, Function, Order of Cosmos. Wisdom simply means conscious control of our activities.

Conscious control of activities means keeping our efforts in line with our desired objectives. In order to do this one must know what one truly wants and what that one is doing in the now.

Try to experience that Wisdom now. Consider something that you want in your life. When you have it in mind, try to keep it in mind. At the same time, try to relax and observe yourself very carefully.

This two-fold activity creates a kind of power circuit between ourselves and our objectives. Keeping conscious of both in the now subtly aligns our forces with the manifestation of our fulfillment.

It is the alignment of our forces with the manifestation of our fulfillment that is essentially what we mean by Wisdom.

Notice the connection between The Crown and Wisdom on the Tree. The Crown represents the Quest for Truth, piercing the veil with our awareness, seeing into ever clearer, larger dimensions of the true nature of what is. Wisdom means aligning our forces with the manifestation of our fulfillment.

This alignment depends upon developing awareness to the level of Truth Consciousness. To truly **SEE** what we are doing with our forces in the now, and to Truly Know what we **WANT** develops as a result of *trying* to see, to be aware of what is.

Our level of perception grows and develops into ever

clearer awareness of vibrations through the steady effort to be more aware. But that effort is not easy to carry on. As was stated in the last chapter, just try to practice it continually all day and you will discover how often you forget, how little you actually, intentionally **DO** it.

And it is the same with Wisdom. Being intentionally Wise is a new way of life that requires the ending of old habits. We are in the habit of **NOT** trying to be conscious in the Light of True Perception, of **NOT** intentionally remaining aware of our goals and what we are doing.

But little by little, through applied effort, the new way of living develops. Eventually, it requires less discipline to stay aware of ourselves. It is this way with our work on all ten Spheres. Our ability to live in these new ways **CONSISTENTLY** will grow as we make the effort to apply them as consistently as we possibly can.

Let us try to apply Wisdom right now relative to our awakening to our True Divine Nature, our Higher Self within. First, try to calmly sense and feel your awareness joining you to that True Self, the Divine Light or Spark you truly **ARE**. Remaining calm and relaxed, begin to sense the goal.

As you do this, observe yourself very carefully in the now. Observe what is happening with your attention, your thoughts, any feelings or vibrations within you. Consciously observe what your body is doing, any movements, like your breathing. Feel your posture. Just stay as conscious of yourself overall in the now as you possibly can.

Now see if you can keep both in consciousness. Be aware of your goal of awakening to your True Divine Nature, and observe yourself carefully in the now. This is applying Wisdom to your awakening. Wisdom is a powerful, creative force that we can always rely upon to produce the results we need. Those results do not often come all at once. But if we are patient and persistent in our application of Wisdom to our goal, it will manifest.

Things do not often happen when we want them to. But they always happen when they are really needed to.

When we are **NOT** aware of a goal, and **NOT** observing ourselves in the now, we are **NOT** applying Wisdom.

To apply Wisdom to the earth plane, our worldly needs, the same procedure is to be followed. Simply become aware of something you feel you want or need on the material level. With that in mind, carefully observe yourself in the now.

Wisdom is a moment by moment kind of practice. There is no one thing that Wisdom should be applied to. It is to be applied to all our wants and needs.

No needs or desires are wrong, as long as we fulfill them in a balanced, conscious, decent manner. Our desires for Truth Consciousness are really no higher than our desire, say, for sexual fulfillment. It is when we allow one desire to run us at the expense of another, blocking and frustrating that other, that difficulty ensues.

Let us try to apply Wisdom to this way of whole and balanced living. Become aware of something you desire in your life that you would consider to be of a worldly nature. When you have that in mind, begin to consider the goal. In other words, try to sense what the fulfillment of that desire would be like. Watch yourself carefully during this exercise. Keep your sense of fulfillment whole and balanced and harmonious.

There **IS** a way to satisfy our deepest desires without sacrificing our higher, "spiritual" natures and pursuits. By trying to sense that experience of balanced (Beauty) fulfillment (Victory), and staying aware of ourselves in the now, we are applying Wisdom to that solution. And Wisdom never fails.

Wisdom is our most reliable business partner. Call to mind a particular challenge, goal, or problem facing you relative to your business, job, or career. When you have it in mind, work on becoming aware of the experience of the solution. How would it feel if you reached that goal? Try to sense or "tune in" to the experience of the situation being transformed in line with your needs. At the same time, remain aware of yourself in the now.

By staying conscious of our goals and ourselves in the now, we begin to notice when we are wasting attention, time, or energy on other matters. This keeps us focused on our objectives and we begin doing what we can to reach them. Wisdom produces results.

While Wisdom is the way out of every difficulty and the way into ultimate fulfillment, it is not always so easy or pleasant to apply. It means keeping the attention from drifting aimlessly. In the now, it has got to be focused on what we want and what we are doing. To be Wise is to be doing all we can for what we want in the now.

We are always doing. Activity, emotion, thoughts, feelings, desire, attitudes radiate constantly from us. Wisdom means being conscious of these and directing them to serve our purposes. We do not automatically work in our own best interest. We have to watch ourselves constantly in order to keep ourselves in line.

We embarass people with our speech, hurt them with our feelings, lose touch with them with our thinking, upset them with our actions. And through it all, ASSUME we are conscious and under Wise self control.

Wisdom is the key to happy relationships. Right now, consider one important individual in your life. Or, you may feel there is no one close to you and are experiencing loneliness. In that case, try becoming aware of the kind of relationship you want.

While doing this, stay self aware in the now. Enter a

state of balanced harmony with that other individual. Try to feel an inner sense of building a good, strong, harmonious relationship. Stay aware of the other and yourself and you will automatically begin to sense the right state to work yourself into in the now.

That is Wisdom applied to relationships, but look at how much effort it takes to actually do it. Unless we are making an intentional effort to actually **BE** Wise in the now relative to a particular goal, you can be sure that we are **NOT** doing it.

Wisdom can also be applied relative to our entire life in general. Right now, just try to get a sense of how you want your life to go and grow. Try to sense the state of fulfillment in general. As you are working on becoming aware of this general goal, carefully observe yourself in the now. You will find your forces, your inner vibrations, becoming subtly aligned with the manifestation of that objective.

Wisdom is the conscious linking of our self in the now with our goals or objectives. Through this conscious linking our energies begin to circulate in line with our needs in a balanced, natural manner.

Wisdom is absolutely essential for our success in business, romance, or any large or important venture. The daily linking of ourselves with our goals in consciousness awakens us to new and deeper levels of what is happening and how better to align our forces with the manifestation of our ultimate fulfillment.

As soon as we notice a strong desire in daily life, that is the time to apply Wisdom to its conscious, whole, harmonious and decent fulfillment. As larger, more important goals or needs make themselves evident, we can intentionally focus more of our attention, time, and energy on those, and let smaller, less important (to us) wants slide. It is all a matter of choice based on what we find we truly want most deeply.

Sometimes we feel we do not know **WHAT** we truly want. The remedy for this is simple. Just observe yourself carefully for a day and you will discover all sorts of little desires flaring up. Pause to look more closely at these. Try to get in touch with the peace and joy of their fulfillment without stress or strain. Stay aware of yourself in the now as you do this. That is applying Wisdom to small desires.

This process gradually leads to the discovery of deeper needs and wants, going all the way to our sense of our True Purpose which **MUST** be fulfilled. That is because we gradually get more in touch with ourselves through this process, until we realize **WHO WE REALLY ARE.**

And that is where Wisdom leads. That is where it can take us, as we apply it.

SPHERE 3:
UNDERSTANDING

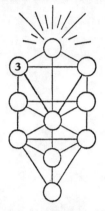

By now, the meaning of the title of this book may be clearer. Qabala's principle value is guiding us to Inner Freedom. Inner Freedom means the control and intelligent direction of our forces, as opposed to the Inner Slavery or Bondage of having to **REACT** automatically, unconsciously, and futiley to the events and circumstances of our daily lives.

The Qabala Tree of Life shows us **WHAT TO DO WITH OUR ENERGIES** in the now, for advancing into the Light of Truth. It is in that Light, called Noetic, that we can see our own True Nature, the True Nature of our present circumstances, and what we can do to Truly expand upon our Fulfillment.

It is this progress into Light, ever more Light, that is the purpose of our lives. Every pain, joy, desire, and experience has been to subtly and gradually guide us in the quest for True Fulfillment. Only as we clarify, sharpen, and develop our Perceptive Awareness, until it finally pierces the veil and responds to Noetic Light Frequencies, can we Fulfill our purpose and our True Selves.

Sphere number three on the Tree is named Understanding. Understanding of what is happening and how to respond is a far more reliable guide for success and happiness than blindly taking chances.

Understanding is a dangerous function. We suffer when we rely upon **FALSE** Understanding. And relying upon **FALSE** Understanding is the **ONLY** cause of suffering.

True Understanding means conscious, perceptive insight that is helpful and constructive. That is the only type of Understanding worth having or experiencing in the now.

False Understanding means relying on mere logic to justify what we do, when doing that only gets us into deeper trouble. For example, we can look at life and consider the pains attendant upon living. It is easy to say that pain in any form is unfair, bad, not good. We can easily justify that point of view by saying that we did not choose to live, we did not mean to hurt anyone, therefore it is not just that we should be hurt by life.

How many times have we been hurt and felt that it was not fair? How often have we experienced anger and frustration at a grievous loss or brutal form of opposition? Too often. This demonstrates wrong or **FALSE** Understanding. Why? Because indulging in that point of view only makes things **WORSE.**

One definition of Right Understanding is Understanding that is helpful, constructive, increasing our power, improving our attitude, bringing meaning and Beauty into our lives.

True Understanding harmonizes the being and integrates our functions into success and higher accomplishment. It is a state of conscious living and conscious function, a state of Conscious Being that we can train and develop ourselves to be able to "tune into" and *feel* **AT WILL.**

Understanding is the conscious, balanced, harmonious state of penetrative insight into what is happening and what to do about it in line with the fulfillment of our True Self and True Purpose.

Feel and enter that state now. You can if you try. Relax, take a long deep breath, and become aware of yourself. Feel your present state consciously. Observe the vibrations, the energy currents, the feelings and drives circulating through your being. That is always the first step to tuning into a particular Cosmic Vibration or whole and balanced *frequency*: self-awareness.

Now try to sense what is really happening to you in the now, even as you continue reading. And observe what you are doing, trying to clearly sense, feel, know, perceive what is really going on in the now.

At this point, try to sense what you can really do about **WHAT IS**, in line with your True Needs for peace, happiness, contentment.

That is all there is to it. Understanding is a state, a functional state of being, to be practiced, experienced and applied. The more we remember to do that, the easier it becomes and the deeper we can go.

True Understanding is a state of conscious, functional interaction with the coordinates of a particular situation or set of circumstances. When we enter that state we enter a Cosmic Ray of order and Light.

Choose a particular situation in your life which you are presently concerned about. Something difficult or important to you which you want to handle well.

With that situation in mind, try to enter the ray of True Understanding. First, try to feel innerly balanced, calm, at peace and aware. Then enter the state of clearly seeing what is going on, what you are doing in the now, and what you can do to really help the situation work out as you want it to.

Understanding is our sanctuary, the place we need to go to figure things out. From Understanding we emerge with reliable knowledge of what is happening and how to respond.

Understanding is a state free from stress, unhappiness, and delusion. That last condition, *delusion*, is one deserving of further explanation. To be deluded is the mental or intellectual aspect of False Understanding.

When we **THINK** we know what is really happening, and **THINK** we know what we are doing, and **THINK** we know what we can do about it **AND ARE WRONG**, then we are **DELUDED**. This is very common, and the cause of nearly every single frustration in our lives.

A common example of delusion is the worker who figures out a clever way to tackle a job. But on going about it, finds that his notion was overly complicated, time consuming, and costly. Parents do this when they decide on a way to protect and care for their children that is very logical but completely out of touch with the real inner needs for self-expression of that child.

How do we avoid the grievous error of deluding ourselves into believing that things are as they are not? How do we avoid wasting our precious time, energy, and income on false schemes and impossible dreams? Through work on **CONSCIOUSNESS** In True Understanding.

Try to enter that ray now. Feel the calm state of conscious insight into what is really happening in the now, what you are presently doing, feeling, thinking, and what you **CAN** do to bring about what you truly want. Enter that experience now, and as you do, be very very **CONSCIOUS**. Carefully observe your state, how you are feeling, what is happening.

As we work on awareness in that ray, we soon are able to sense when we are in a false substitute, an imposter ray, the ray of self-**DELUSION**.

The signs that we are misinterpreting, misevaluating, mistaken about what *is* are many. The first is the subtle **FEELING** of being impractical, overly idealistic and theoretical relative to what is. You can feel that state now if you try. Try to feel the inner sense of fooling or deceiving yourself. Try to feel a sense of being unrealistic, too intellectual and ungrounded, identified with false and unfounded ideas about what is real. That is a ray, a state we can feel, observe and recognize when it is upon us.

Now, try to feel the opposite. Try to feel the sense of being completely integrated and perfectly interacting in the reality of what is. That is part of the state of Understanding. The more we enter it, the easier it is to enter and the deeper and more penetrating our state of awareness grows.

In that state of conscious and balanced interconnection make the effort to be more clearly aware, to more deeply penetrate into the reality of what *is* with your perceptive cognition (seeing and knowing without thinking).

Balance, relaxation, and feeling strength and harmony are signs of the True state of Understanding. When we are feeling nervous, intense, overly enthused or depressed or even tired, True Understanding cannot be assimilated by our consciousness.

Right now, let us work our way into that balanced, relaxed state. Take a nice full breath and try to sense Understanding's energies, vibrations, flowing deeply within and throughout your being. Feel your way into peace, strength and a harmonious, alert state. Little by little, the more we practice entering, living, and trying to remain in that state, the greater our power to do it at will shall grow.

Understanding is a ray we can enter as we develop the inner freedom to *not* automatically, blindly react to circumstances. This develops as we actually make the effort to gain harmonious, practical, useful insight into what is really happening, what we are doing in the now, and what we can usefully do to meet our needs for a happy life.

Let us try one more exercise, and apply it to a relationship. Consider one individual who is important in your life. When you have that one in your mind, calmly direct awareness to yourself as well. Try to relax, look for any tensions, stress, or other signs of discord or unbalance and release them.

Now, with that individual in mind, try to sense more clearly and truly what is happening in your relationship. Who and what that other really is, you are, and both of your needs. Try to sense, feel, penetrate into what is real and true and essential.

During this, watch your own state carefully, observing what you are doing, feeling, thinking, or paying attention to.

Calmly enter the strong and balanced ray of Truly Conscious Understanding of what you can do in your relationship with that other to meet your needs.

Little by little, by taking time to actually dwell in Understanding, ideas and insights, creative, useful guidance unfold in our conscious minds. We then have a reliable course of action to test out in that particular context.

Understanding is the powerful, extremely powerful means of directing ourselves, handling relationships, jobs, careers, or our business in line with our purpose.

As we rely upon it more and more, our perception unfolds, and we shall taste the **OMNILUCENT NOETIC LIGHT**, the superconscious **MIND-LEVEL** state of our True or Higher Self at The Crown.

Let us now try to apply that powerful ray, the ray of Functional Understanding, directly to our development into Higher Conscious Beings. First, relax and become clearly, calmly, and fully self-aware. Then, consider the goal, the achievement of the state of True Awareness in Light. Observe your present activities, what you are doing, radiating, feeling. Observe your mind and what you are doing with your attention.

Now, try to sense what it is you need to do in order to experience more of that goal, the True Light in your own consciousness. In other words, let us work our way into the state of Understanding what we can do to advance, to experience and feel and live in more Light right now.

Sometimes we are not only concerned with what we can do for ourselves **NOW**, but also **LATER**. In other words, assume you have a business meeting tomorrow and want to know how to handle it **THEN,** when you are there. To receive this type of Understanding as a guide, the same technique is applied. Simply make the effort to enter the state of Understanding, of clear and exact knowing, of just what you need to do then to make it turn out as you truly want.

When we are angry, reacting, triggering off, confused, Understanding cannot enter. As long as we are feeling sorry for ourselves or complaining about things, we cannot receive the guiding light of Understanding and discover how to respond to what *is* for our good.

Understanding is the key to changing any experience into one that is useful, worthwhile, harmonious. It is **OUR** responsibility to relate with what *is* for good results. To wait for circumstances to be the way we want without our making the necessary effort to relate with them practically and harmoniously is to fail our cosmic responsibility and that is vain and worse than useless.

Therefore, when something happens that triggers us off, the first thing to do is become conscious and enter a harmonious state of balance and order. Enter that balanced state before doing anything about the situation.

As we work on entering the state of order, awareness, and harmony, we are gaining inner freedom. We gain more as we utilize every experience of pain, opposition, or resistance to our desires to exercise and work on **NOT** blindly reacting, but instead, practicing as best we can going directly into the calm and conscious state of Understanding to guide our responses.

Working on ourselves in this way, in time, we treat all obstacles as opportunities to grow. And as we work on dealing with all things from the state of Understanding, we grow in insight, peace, and power as our needed objectives are achieved.

SPHERE 4:
MERCY

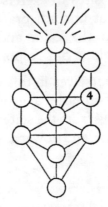

We are dynamic energy beings in a dynamic energy universe. The energy of the universe flows through us, into us, from us. And we are responsible for how we transform it.

The Qabala Tree of Life shows us ten different ways of receiving and expressing the cosmic energy flow. Each sphere represents a level of consciousness we can animate with the cosmic flow in order to fulfill our True Natures.

Not only ourselves, but our projects, business, and relationships each have their own True Nature. There is a structure, function and order to our every goal. By applying our force in the forms designated by the Spheres on the Tree, we can fulfill the True Needs of our goals for their whole, balanced, and nourishing manifestation.

The fourth Sphere on the Qabala Tree of Life is named Mercy. This Sphere represents the forces and states of ease, gentleness, and gratification. To a certain degree, our health, happiness, and intelligence require Mercy in the now.

Let us make the effort to feel the power of Mercy, and to measure just how much of it brings us harmony and balance in the present. Take a long, slow breath, and become aware of yourself. Observe your feelings, become aware of your body, relax. Now feel a sense of ease, gentleness, and release flowing through your being.

Mercy, like the other energies or *vibratory frequencies* represented by the Tree, can be tuned into by ourselves when we go through the process just described. The more attention we give to those feelings of ease, gentleness, and release, the stronger they flow.

But, as with all forces, Mercy is dangerous. If we give ourselves too much of it, we begin to "space out", lose touch with what we are doing. There is such a thing as letting go **TOO MUCH,** being **INSUFFICIENTLY** vigilant, alert, and aware.

Mercy, therefore, needs an anchor. And that anchor is the awareness of our needs and goals.

Bring to mind a specific goal or objective you have in your life. When you have that in mind, **THEN** tune into Mercy. Keeping aware of that particular goal, observe the energy currents of ease, gentleness, freedom, and unforced expansion flowing and growing within you.

As long as we remain aware of what is going on in the present relative to our goals and needs, we can experience as much Mercy as we want **SAFELY.** Right now, while reading, become aware of what is happening in the present. Without losing track of what you are reading, sense, feel, notice and observe the conditions and activities of your present here-now environment.

Now add to that an awareness of yourself. Observe your feelings, become aware of your body and release any tensions in it. Notice your breathing, and what you are doing with your attention in the now.

See if you can now blend those two applications of your awareness. While reading, maintain awareness of yourself and what is happening around you. Actually practicing this strengthens and develops our perceptive faculties. In time, we pick up vibrations of *order* and *truth* which guide us better than mere logic, opinions, or emotional impulse ever could. Then, in time, we awaken to the Light of True Perception.

The important thing is to practice that awareness of what *is*, for that practice and the discipline to do it produces the results we seek.

It is when we are practicing this awareness of self in the here-now that we are to become aware of a particular need or goal we want to meet. Try that now. We have already done it many times during the course of this book. Become aware of self in the here-now, and a goal, desire, or need you want to meet.

Within the context of that state of awareness, bring the energy currents of Mercy into play. Then we are anchored.

We cannot disregard our own stress limitations and get away with it. Mercy is like a steam release valve.

But if too much pressure is released, there will be insufficient power to drive the engines, focus our forces, and fulfill our needs and purpose.

In the now, stay in touch with your stress level of pressure. Bring in just enough peace and ease to remain harmonious, balanced, and aware.

Taking a full, slow breath and giving the back of our necks a good rub is one way to *ease up*. Try that now. And follow it with calmly sensing the ease of peace and harmony flowing into and from you.

Mercy is an essential ingredient for relationships we want to work, grow, or last. We cannot be easy enough on others unless we are easy enough on ourselves. We tend to drive others as hard as we drive ourselves.

What happens when we are too demanding with someone? Either they break under our pressure, rebel, or just leave us. Millions are being tortured daily by pushy, frustrated, belligerent lovers, parents, friends.

We do not mean to hurt others. But it cannot be helped as long as we are ourselves out of balance. So we owe it, not just to ourselves, but to the others in our life whom we care about and need to work with, to become balanced in the vibrations of Mercy.

We can measure the needs of Mercy in a particular relationship. In so doing, we can correct or remedy any imbalance. Let us try that now. Bring to mind one individual, or a group of individuals, with whom you have or want an important relationship.

With attention on that other, become aware of how you yourself are feeling in the now. Look for any signs of stress or strain within you. Begin to feel a sense of Mercy, of letting the pressure release.

As we remain conscious of that other individual during this exercise, we will sense when we are being overly Merciful, or not Merciful enough. The key is what has been termed *focused relaxation*. If we are feeling a loss of focused, clear awareness of that other's state in the now, if we are feeling like we are drifting, "spacing out", or losing our sharp, clear sense of practicality, it means we are being overly Merciful. If we are feeling unneccessarily hard, angry, frustrated, blocked or demanding, it means we need to spend more time consciously releasing the pressure in ourselves.

Focused relaxation is when we feel keenly aware and responsible, without discordant stress, strain, or nervousness.

Just by considering the Mercy aspect in a given relationship, we are working on a factor of major importance. Take a moment to consider another relationship you have or want, and study it to see if you have been too demanding, too hard, uselessly and unnecessarily insistent, angry, or inflexible.

It is a worthwhile practice to regularly consider our

important relationships to see whether we are applying too much or too little Mercy. We can then experiment with a bit more or less to see how that affects the relationship.

If we are to meet our goals, we cannot be too hard on ourselves. If we make the process excessively unpleasant and sacrificial, we will either give up before we accomplish it, or burn out, break down, fall ill in our efforts.

Measuring the Mercy factor in our actions, avoiding excessive stress and strain, could avoid many surgeries, the need for pills, treatments, etc. Also, by living in an easier, more harmonious and comfortable manner, we find less of a need to overcompensate for our stresses with excessive indulgences such as overeating, over sleeping, over drinking. It even brings in balance and healthful harmony to one's sexual drives. These tend to increase for some or dry up for others when they force themselves to work and push extremely.

Mercy is a delicious energy frequency we can feel right now. Let us do so. Tune into Mercy in a conscious, grounded, anchored state. And take that state with you into your daily activities and situations. When a crisis or opportunity arises, paying attention to the degree of stress and strain we are allowing to get to us is a great protection.

In the balanced, Merciful state, carefully observe what is happening to you. Do you not sense a field of order generating within you and radiating from you. This ordered field keeps our faculties sharp and cool so that we can work at our highest potential. It also penetrates into our environment as an ordering, cooling, harmonizing influence.

The more we practice dwelling in Mercy **CONSCIOUSLY** and in balanced focus, the more it grows and the more we can handle. Little by little, we thus learn how to handle even the most challenging of situations with cool and efficient poise and good sense. Life becomes an easier and more pleasant experience for us. And that makes us easier and more pleasant for others to relate with.

We thrive and flourish in our lives by how well we relate with our fellow beings. As we awaken to and satisfy their true needs, we find harmony and cooperation, much needed additional power to achieve our goals and satisfy our own needs. Whether you are a business person, a parent, a healer, or all three, everyone we come in contact with needs, requires, must have a certain measure of Mercy from us. Exactly how much and in what form will be revealed at the time through the practice of being conscious of self and other, in tune with Mercy.

As we work on making our lives, relationships, businesses and growth process more consciously Merciful, we are attuning ourselves to the experience of inner and outer abundance. This is something that has been proven over and over, and we can prove it for ourselves.

By being overly hard and demanding upon ourselves and others, we actually repel all the richness we are striving for. As we work in balance, consciously and measuredly attuned to Mercy, the flowers of a higher, richer life bloom gently and gradually, yet strongly and with stability.

The higher faculties of perceptive awareness, culminating in our birth into Noetic Light, cannot function or be cultivated in an overly stressful, ruthless state. Intunement to Mercy allows our True Self to unfold and freely fulfill our Cosmic Mission in **REALITY**, in **LIGHT, IN TRUTH.**

As a final exercise on Mercy, let us apply it directly to our quest for Light, the True Perceptive Level. Become aware of the energy currents, the state, the feelings of

Mercy's peace and ease flowing within. With awareness of that state, that mode of gentle, balanced function, try to **SEE** what *is* in the now.

Realize that there are higher, truer levels of awareness of what is happening and what we need to do relative to our present set of circumstances than we are currently enjoying. That is always the case. There is always a higher, larger, truer level of awareness to attain.

As we make the effort to be more clearly, consciously aware, to pierce the veil of the limits of our present state we eventually enter the Noetic Light. There, our True Self is conscious of the True Nature of the Cosmic Process in the **NOW**.

By staying conscious of our level or degree of Mercifulness relative to our efforts and objectives, we hasten our progress into the limitless **LIGHT** of Ultimate Fulfillment.

SPHERE 5:
SEVERITY

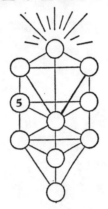

We each have much to do, much to accomplish. The ability to take care of all the details of daily life calmly and efficiently is itself a great achievement.

All too often our emotions interfere. This is not to say that emotions are bad or useless. But they have their place, their function. Activities requiring keen insight and step-by-step activity have no place for emotional excitability.

When we mix or confuse levels, when we emote when we should be thinking and think when we need to be acting, we create inner turmoil for ourselves which effectively blocks our smooth, efficient handling of the coordinates of our present situation.

The intelligent measure and control of our forces is part of the function represented by the fifth Sphere on the Qabala Tree of Life. This is the Sphere of Severity.

Severity is the cool, keen state of focused activity, effort or will. Right now, try to feel a sense of being fully integrated into the structure, function, order of your life. Take a full breath, relax, and feel the sense of oneness with the smooth effective flowing of the activities fulfilling your needs.

Severity means seeing what needs to be done and doing it, step-by-step. It is the cool, calculating state of the expert. He or she has a job, knows what is needed for its efficient execution, and does it in the succinct sequence of steps.

In the now, sense that coolness, that poise, that methodical certainty and precision. This should feel like a healing, harmonizing, refreshing state. It is not negative or positive emotionally. The feelings are balanced, neutral, not blocked or repressed. Feel the mind sharp, clear, mathematical, practical.

Severity is the state of "drawing the line" on what you will allow. This is a precise, mathematical operation, "drawing the line", necessary for fulfilling our structural needs and limitations.

Severity is an essential element for True Perception and Achievement. Have you ever felt inundated with the build-up of pressures? You know, when duties keep piling up and it seems there are just not enough hours in the day to do all that needs doing.

Severity is a great relief at such times. At such times, our emotions have a nack for getting involved. Tension, anxiety, fear, panic and hysteria result from trying to accomplish with our emotions what they are not designed to do. By entering the state of cool and keen Severity, the emotions are cooled, and the mind can pick out the efficient, systematic way of tackling the details in an intelligent, responsible sequence.

Let us try that now. Bring to mind something in your

life which needs doing; some project requiring your attention or responsibility demanding your time.

With that in mind, enter the state of Severity. Take a nice full breath and bring the emotions into a cool, neutral, UNintense state. Then, feel your mind tuning up into a finely functional, mathematically precise instrument.

Now, consider your pressing project. Calmly break it down into the sequence of steps for its accomplishment. Throughout this process stay extra aware of the emotions to **KEEP THEM OUT OF IT**; stay intentionally neutral and emotionally at peace.

To break something down into its sequence of steps is fairly easy when we are not emotionally involved. For example, assume I have to write a letter to a client but it seems like I just do not have the time. The first thing to do is to take the time to calmly look at the situation as a whole. Then, in my mind or, preferably, on a sheet of paper, write down the steps involved in writing the letter. These might be: 1) find out where my stationary is 2) take some 3) sit down and think of what to say 4) write the letter 5) place it in the envelope 6) address and stamp it 7) mail it off.

There is no place in that sequence for getting worked up, panicking, fearing the worst, shouting at my secretary, feeling frustration, etc. I now have the simple step-by-step process or plan for accomplishing my job.

Once one job is planned out, then plan out the sequence of steps for the other matters demanding accomplishment. This may seem like a waste of time when all these things need doing as soon as possible. In fact, however, it saves time. It also brings the emotions under control and brings a new level of ease and harmony into our efficient operations.

It is astonishing to witness the total transformation of

one's own emotional state as a result of entering Severity. What had before been eating away at us, forcing us to shout at people without their really deserving it, etc. now becomes interesting, enjoyable functions leading to the fulfillment of our responsibilities and establishing of our lives on a higher plane.

Let us now try dealing with several jobs or functions. First, list the basic things you have to take care of in your present life sitation. It is not necessary to wait until we are feeling overwhelmed by demands or opportunities to enter and apply Severity.

Once you have your basic list, break each item down to a practical, realistic sequence of steps leading to accomplishment.

Sometimes, we do not know how to accomplish what must be done. At such a point we usually start to panic or complain. Instead, enter the cool, keen state of Severity. Then, simply break down the process of **FINDING OUT WHAT TO DO** into an orderly and unstrained series of steps.

An important point to remember for finding the right **SEQUENCE** is to first *tune into* the vibrations of Severity. Relax, cool the emotions, feel a sense of calm, free-flowing expertise, precision and methodicalness.

Let us more thoroughly explore the difference between blocking feelings of frustration and cooling the emotions. They are definitely not the same. Right now, *feel* your way into a neutral condition of balance. Feel neither positive nor negative, for nor against. Just feel inner peace, serenity, combined with a sharp, clear state of alertness.

Cooling the emotions is **NOT** repressing the emotions or drives. To bring the emotions into a state of natural, healthy balance, begin by observing the present emotional state. Can you feel your feelings in the now?

Try. Direct attention to your inner self and sense whatever feelings, mood, attitude or desires may be subtly present.

Just doing this brings about an emotional balance. It takes attention **OFF** whatever situation is triggering the emotions, and directs it **TO** the emotional state itself. Some soft, full breathing and relaxing any physical tensions in the body helps a good deal as well.

The emotional level of Severity is therefore a cool, calm peace - **NOT** hard ignoring of our finer feelings and sensibilities.

Let us enter and dwell in that state. When we combine with it a sense of keen, functional, methodical integration with the necessary functions of our lives, we enter Severity more deeply. Then, from that **STATE** of cool methodicalness, analyze something that you must do or accomplish. Break it down into the step-by-step process you will follow for its efficient accomplishment.

The final phase of Severity is the actual *doing* of the sequence. The same cool, keenly alert state is to be applied during this *activity* phase. In calm peace, step-by-step even the lengthiest, most complicated situations or projects can be mastered in good time.

Severity is most helpful in relationships. Bring to mind a particular individual in your personal life, or perhaps choose one individual you have to work with on your job. With that individual in mind, enter the cool, calm, unforced state of conscious Severity. Try to become aware of what you need to do, of the step-by-step process of handling that relationship properly.

This exercise helps us develop a deeper, impersonal level to our relationship. No matter how close we are to someone, a certain level of impersonality is essential. Even a mother and child must share more than emotion - charged, deeply personal feelings toward one another. There needs to be a level where both can detach, cool it, to see clearly and exactly what **NEEDS** to be done for the real good of both. If we only react to each other, insisting on doing just what we want, driven blindly by our emotions, our relationships degenerate into soggy messes of brutal selfishness, demanding and greed.

That detachment which accompanies the state of Severity in a relationship often feels quite refreshing, especially when applied to our most intimate ones. It gives us a chance to see more clearly what we need to do to keep things on a truly healthy and harmonious course.

Severity connects us to something in us that is higher than our personalities. It connects our consciousness to our **INDIVIDUALITY**. Our **INDIVIDUALITY** can be defined as the actual needs of our True Structures. While our personalities are the conglomeration of our acquired and habitualized likes and dislikes, mental associations, unchecked expectations and customs.

Severity also enables us to observe the True Needs of the **INDIVIDUALITIES** of those others we deal with.

Thus, the application of Severity to our life leads us to higher levels of Perceptive Cognition.

It is only in the Highest, relative to the human state, which we call the Noetic or Mind Level (not to be confused with mere intellect or the logical mind), that we See and Know our essential Structure, Function, Order in the Structure, Function, Order of Cosmos. And in that Seeing and Knowing, Fulfill It.

Severity can also be applied directly to the cultivation of our Perceptive Faculties. In other words it can help us to pass through the level of identification with our personalities, into the Enlightened state of Truly Self-Conscious Individualized Beings.

First, let us enter that ray, that conscious state of Severity. Relax the body, bring coolness and peace to the emotions, and sharpness and clear focus to the mind. Let us now feel that state gently flowing through us, gradually filling us to the deepest and highest levels.

Then, in that clear, sharp, neutral state, consider the goal. First, we want to go beyond our present level and into a clearer state of awareness of vibrations, sensing and feeling the way things are, our needs, and the way to their accomplishment. From that level, which we can call Conscious Vibrational Attunement, Intuitive Awareness, early sensings of Individualization, etc. we pass into Noetic Light. Here, we consciously register Light or Mind Frequencies, and See and Know our Selves most Truly, and our Purpose in the Cosmic Process.

Those are the three steps. It is a sequence of passage from sensory, logical, emotional identification. We gradually function more and more consciously with intunement to vibrations of Truth and Order, Wholeness and Balanced Harmony. From reliance upon that intuitive awareness we ultimately enter Light's Regions, the lowest level of which is named Noetic Light.

In your present state of Severity, consider that process, and begin to sense the state of perfect functional integration within it.

The fruits of Severity do not happen all at once. Tuning into its ray produces results, however, and those unfold in naturally timed order or sequence themselves. Little-by-little, insight enters our minds and we see what to do; structural power patterns our functioning and we find ourselves doing it.

That is how we can patiently, effectively accomplish all the many things in our lives that need doing. Through the conscious application of Severity, step-by-step, we achieve and fulfill, progress and ascend, into *infinity*.

SPHERE 6:
BEAUTY

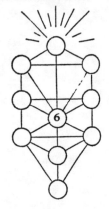

The general pattern of the Qabala Tree of Life demonstrates profound intelligence. What better force to follow and temper Severity than Beauty!

On the Tree, each Sphere represents one **PART** of the whole state of consciousness we can label Truly Enlightened Function or Being. Spheres follow Spheres on the Tree, the way layers follow layers in the structure of a pyramid. Each layer adds new depth and meaning to the preceding one. Each Sphere compensates for, and expands upon, the balance and order of the Sphere which came before.

The fact that every Sphere is connected tells us that none are to stand or be applied alone. Their numerical sequence illustrates the Natural Order process of their emergence from one another.

Whether we are working on building a house or a business, a higher conscious state or a relationship with someone close, the forces represented by the ten Spheres of the Tree show us how to do it, and how it must be done.

Qabala, then, offers us something we are not taught in schools today. Qabala teaches us **HOW TO LIVE.**

Living is not new, nor is the established science and art of it. Ancients knew the basics of how it can and must be done to fulfill our purpose individually and collectively. That knowledge is termed The Gnosis, and Qabala is one of its representatives, teaching us the whole and balanced way to success and fulfillment, cosmic order and Noetic Light.

The sixth Sphere on the Tree of Life is named Beauty. Beauty is a state of joy, inspiration, harmony. It is an **EXPERIENCE** we can **FEEL.** Two individuals can listen to a given song on the radio. One of them finds the song Beautiful, the other does not. The Beauty is not in the song, *but in the one the song triggered it off in.* While we may not find Beauty in the same things, we can certainly tell, if we observe carefully, when one is **GETTING BEAUTY FROM SOMETHING.** Their eyes sparkle, their voice softens, they are radiant with strength, vitality and peace.

The function of art is to teach us what we are capable of. We go to the movies, for example, to re-kindle raptures, moods, and attitudes that we are feeling hungry for.

The function of the Gnosis, and specifically Qabala, is to teach us how we can experience and manifest the states and conditions we need without having to depend upon outer stimuli to "get it".

By placing Beauty on the Tree, Qabalists tell us that it is a state we can tune into, feel, express and experience **AT WILL.**

Do that now. Relax, take a deep, slow breath, and tune into the state or experience of true and total Beauty. Feel as you do when you hold the one you love, when all seems right with yourself and the world, when you feel in tune and at one with your True Self and in harmony with the whole Cosmic Process.

That is how we can make this a Beautiful moment.

Beauty is not impractical. In fact, it is false,

transient pleasure masquerading as Beauty which leads to our harm.

Wherever we are, there is a way to feel Beauty, to be in harmony with what is happening, in a safe, realistic, practical way.

While reading this, enter that balanced state. Become consciously aware and alert in the now. At the same time, feel in harmony, fulfilled, in a purely Beautiful state. Beauty is a **WAY** of doing what must be done.

And it is an **ESSENTIAL** ingredient to a happy life. Beauty intunes us to our Individuality. Pleasure which masquerades as Beauty only enslaves us to our false or superficial personality.

In the ancient wisdom teachings, we are told that we are essentially eternal, birthless, ageless, deathless beings. But that is only on the individualized level. Our personalities, our likes and dislikes, habits, customs, and opinions are all temporary and doomed.

When one begins to "Tread The Path" to the Heights, one goes to work on **CHANGING** the personality to be more in line and fit the needs of the True Individualizing Self. That is, one works on getting in tune and in conscious touch with his real, structural, cosmic needs, and brings the personality's functions and states into line with those.

Beauty, living in it and working on experiencing more, intunes us to that Individualizing Self. Beauty transcends pleasure and pain. There is a Beauty in suffering, sacrifice, discipline and effort. The experience of Beauty is actually the state of relative at-one-ment (atonement) with the Individual, Conscious Energy Being we are in Fact.

So Beauty is most certainly **NOT** skin deep. But forms, images and sensations can help us discover the experience. We can sense our intunement with the deeper levels of being right now. Begin by relaxing, and directing attention within. Sense, gently feel whatever feelings or vibrations are present.

Now, in an unforced way, expand and deepen awareness to a sense of the Conscious Energy Field, the Real Individual you are which has been hidden by the mask of personality.

This begins as a vague sort of sensing. Add to it a feeling of harmony with that level. Experience a real inner sense of Beauty, peace and love. Not a personal love. Pure love. Not love of anyone or anything in particular. Just Love.

Love and Beauty are the same. Both words represent the state of consciously aligning with an Individual's structure, function, order. That is why sometimes love seems to hurt. We often have to do or accept unpleasant things for those we love. We have to grow, sharpen our faculties, improve our skills in order to better serve the real needs of our Selves and the Selves of others. Love and true service are also one.

Just as we live on the level of Conscious Individuality ourselves, there is a level of Conscious Individuality for our whole planet. We can sense and intune to that right now. Begin by directing awareness to the feeling of seeing through the *physical body* of the planet, through the personalities of all those whose *bodies* are part of earth's substance. Now sense the finer vibrations, make the inner effort to intune to the Individualizing, true structural needs of the earth as a whole relative to the ongoing growth in consciousness characterizing the entire Cosmic Process.

This can become pretty heavy stuff. We are not mentalizing or intellectualizing here. This constitutes work on entering the deeper levels of knowing, of penetrating the cosmic mysteries. Only as we intune to the overall individualizing process of the Earth can we serve her needs and development.

What is the purpose of the Cosmic Process? First of all, there is one. By working on living and staying in tune with Beauty, that purpose and how to contribute to its fulfillment eventually and gradually unfolds.

For one thing, the purpose can be described as the transfiguration of the cosmos into a field of perfect light. Earth, for example, is not just the soil and the trees. It is the thoughts and consciousness of everyone living and nourished by its energy field. Sense that now. Try to feel the sense of earth being a vast, conscious energy field striving in its sleep for identification with its True Self.

The True Self of the Earth has a structure, function, and order - in other words, a Cosmic Purpose - just as we do. The earth is the collective of the Individualized Field units of you, I, and everyone else alive.

The first purpose of the planet is therefore to awaken to its purpose, and then to fulfill it consciously, working with all the other Individualizing Conscious Energy Fields of the Cosmic Process.

And that purpose, that **COSMIC PURPOSE** can be described as **BEAUTY**.

Beauty is the conscious state of Real and True **FUL-FILLMENT**. It is the product of the union of the Good and the True in Conscious Function and Conscious Being.

Let us try to tune into the Beauty which is the Enlightened Purpose of the whole Cosmic Process. Gently become aware of the vibrations of that limitless condition of harmonious grandeur. It is awesome to even begin to feel. Yet that awesome vibration is nourishing food to our inner beings.

It nourishes our Individualities.

There is a level beyond Individualization. Individualization characterizes the level of Self-Consciousness at the energy field level.

But higher than that is the Noetic Level. Here Individualization has been fulfilled as a phase of development. The intuitive awareness on the vibrational level, which we are basically developing through the practices and procedures described in the present book, have been cultivated to their flowering. When we See and Know in Light's Regions, we become One with the Whole, Light Beings adorned with the Solar Vesture. This is not metaphysics, or theory. It is a scientific, verifiable description of the step-by-step process of the unfoldment of our True Self in Light's Region, the culmination of our development and the purpose of our existence. Every pain, experience, and desire we have known throughout all the aeons of our existence has been for just this reason. That is, for our own Individualization, followed by Birth into the Light.

Beauty, our walking in it and work upon more of it, is the way of awakening to higher levels of Individualization, transcending the death-bound personality and its identification with the physical body.

How do we "walk in Beauty"? It starts by practicing being aware of that inner state of harmony and fulfillment. Little by little we discover that rushing about, speaking too much or too quickly, becoming overly emotional and impatient with things all tends to **DE**-tune us from the state of Beauty, harmony, and fulfillment in the **NOW**.

So that intunement to Beauty becomes a guide. We begin to sense the vibrations of when we are entering a larger field of order and harmony, and when our inner peace and joy are draining.

There are always adjustments we can make to do what needs to be done for practical purposes, and to do it in such a way that Beauty guides, nourishes, and heals us in the process.

Make the effort to feel Beauty now, in all its peace and power within. Enter that state of perfect fulfillment, meaning, love, and inner freedom.

The more attention we give to that experience, the stronger it grows as a guide to a higher, more harmonious future, and a blessing of joy in the now.

We work on bringing more Beauty into our life experience by making it an aspect or function of our goals and objectives.

Let us try that now. Call to mind a particular individual whom you associate with on your job, at work. When you have that one in mind, begin to relax and sense yourself entering a stable, balanced, practical state. Feel on the ball, alert, sharp, skillful, and impersonal.

In that cool, impersonal state (Severity) feel yourself contacting the state of Beauty. But do not lose the practical balance. Beauty is a way of meeting practical necessities. True Beauty will never conflict with our whole and balanced function or handling of responsibilities.

As we sense the way we want to relate with our fellow worker for practical purposes, we can also sense how to do that in a Beautiful, fulfilling, radiantly joyful way.

The same technique is applied for our financial needs, health, closer relationships, and growth into Higher Conscious Cosmic Beings.

Beauty as an experience we can live in and be guided by opens and develops our inner vibratory awareness to True Intunement with our essential, Individualizing Selves.

SPHERE 7:
VICTORY

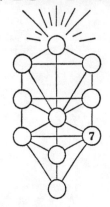

Each Sphere on the Qabala Tree of Life represents a state of consciousness, a way of being and functioning in the now. Verbal definitions and symbolic associations are really secondary. When we are feeling the uplifting vibrations of a given Sphere, and alertly taking care of practical matters in the present, the magnificent value of the Tree of Life is discovered.

These Spheres are energy-stations or power centers in our consciousness. When we are experiencing them, a vivification of our connection with our True Self takes place. We then have new power to develop our abilities and manifest higher fulfillment.

Power and focus are the gifts of each Sphere to the one who knows how to work with them. Some of us feel we are already fulfilled. But that is a passing fancy. Through the conscious application of the Spheres of Qabala we can secure, expand, and develop that fulfillment into dimensions before undreamed of. It is just a matter of contacting the power and focusing it into a given function for a specific result.

This brings us to the seventh Sphere of the Tree, named Victory. Victory represents, in its Qabalistic sense, fulfillment of desire.

Before we can fulfill our desires, we must know what they are. The experience of fulfilling any desire, whatever it may be, brings with it a sense of Victory, Triumph, and Accomplishment.

As we discover and then fulfill our desires, the sense of Victory grows within us. It brings with it deeper levels of security, confidence, inner peace, and satisfaction with life.

So it is not just the satisfaction we experience from the goal being reached, but the sense of Victory and Accomplishment that accompanies it which the Tree points out as being essential.

The first step toward the increase of this essential energy in us is consciously contacting our desires, wants and needs. Right now, become aware of the feelings or vibrations passing through you. Look for any sense of desire, want or need you may be experiencing in the now. This is one way of awakening to new levels of desire within us.

But there are bound to be desires we already are aware of. There is a way we want a particular project to go, a way we want to look and feel, a desire for how we want a certain relationship to progress, etc. In your mind, or on a sheet of paper, make a list of the desires you presently have and are aware of.

This is in itself a very worthwhile practice to do regularly. It often brings with it a deeper realization of desires we have that we have been more or less taking for granted. When we really look at a desire and see what we are wanting, new power and determination for accomplishing it is awakened.

Then go down your list, one item at a time. Pause at each item to feel a sense of Victory relative to it. Try that with one right now. With an awareness of what it is you desire to happen, feel the sense of accomplishment, of being Victorious, relative to it.

That Victorious sense, that feeling of Triumph, Winning, Accomplishment, quickens the flame of our creative power to get the job done. It fills us with encouragement and hope. It is fuel to the fire of our desire and motivation.

With sufficient power and drive, anything can be accomplished. When we tune into Victory relative to a particular desire or need, we increase our drive to attain what we want.

Victory is something we can feel without any particular desire in mind for a kind of general rekindling of our vibrancy. Take a nice, full breath and become aware of how you are feeling in the present. Now, begin to feel the sense of Victory, Triumph, and essentially uplifting accomplishment flowing within and throughout your being.

The control and direction of our attention is crucial to the cultivation of our power centers. Do you not find that a drifting mind or attention blocks the ability to remain tuned into the growing state of Victory?

When working on a particular power on the Tree, within the Self, as soon as you notice that your attention has drifted from the flowing of the force within, simply redirect it. Sometimes we have to go through this procedure of noticing an unintentional drifting and redirecting the focus over and over. Especially when tired, or going through a crisis that is triggering us off, is it difficult to control our attention, to keep it on what we want to grow and happen.

So these are the most dangerous times. When we are tired or upset, and we need Victory to flow in our lives, it is time to diminish or entirely cease speech and activity. The more peaceful and ordered we can remain, the sooner our energy will be replenished and our forces be once again controllable.

Right now, let us feel and enter the ordered, peaceful state of consciousness. Take a slow, full breath, relax, and feel peace and alertness flowing within and throughout. Feel a sense of order, organization, and wholesome, natural peace. Gradually, this settles us down. If you become sleepy or feel drowsiness drawing into you, do not resist the flow of that healing, harmonizing energy. But remain as keenly alert in the present as you can while that healing flow permeates ever more deeply.

Peace and order grow like any other force, as we keep attention on them and do what we can to help them to increase. And this state is itself a kind of Victory, a necessary accomplishment for the adequate handling of any given situation.

Let us now see how the energy of Victory can help us enter a deeply peaceful state of alert order. Become aware of the sense of *accomplishing* peace, calm, and alert awareness. The force of Victory magnetizes us to our goals, to whatever it is we are aware of accomplishing.

So, the force of Victory can help us achieve a state of peace and order, which further aids us to control our attention and keep it on Victory relative to the fulfillment of our other goals.

In the state of peace and alert order, consider one goal, one accomplishment which you have determined you want.

With that in mind, maintain the state of peace and order within, and begin to feel the sense of Victory connected with the fulfillment of that goal.

This is not just an exercise, it constitutes real productive effort and alignment of our creative forces with the manifestation of what we want.

According to Qabala there is never a time when we should not be working if we want to know true peace. But work has many forms, and it is not always intensely active on the more obvious physical levels.

When we practice the state of peace and order in the now, we are working and developing our self-control. When we keep our goals in mind with the sense of Victory, we are deepening and strengthening our attachment to them.

One of the most important things we can do is to carefully watch our energy level in daily living. If we work and push too hard, we will not be able to sustain the focus of our attention when we have time to rest. An uncontrolled attention means we are giving our divine creative energy no direction to work in. Rest means taking things easier, but if we have to totally let go of our deeper drives we have lost balance.

Staying in touch with victory is a necessary part of accomplishment, and constitutes inner work. The true Qabalist, who seeks to go the way of Wisdom into the Light of True Fulfillment based on the ageless and divine science and art of living, alternates rhythmically from outer to inner work, and then from inner to outer.

A very worthwhile practice can be done upon entering sleep and awakening. Each evening, select one want that you have. Bring it to mind in the state of peace and order, and combine that with the sense of Victory associated with what you want to accomplish. As sleepiness and drowsiness set in, for this practice, let them carry you off.

Upon awakening, as soon as possible, select one goal or event you want to manifest, and in peace and order dwell on Victory relative to it. But now, pay special attention to the subtle awakening of vim and vigor and encouragement released by the Victory power center's activation.

Work on this and every power center of Qabala is a wonderful way to exercise. For example, try taking a long walk, staying alertly aware of all that is taking place around you and within you in the now. And during that walk, maintaining the state of peace and order, keep a want in mind and the Victorious sense associated with its fulfillment. This not only aligns and strengthens us relative to our goal, but provides us with greater energy for our exercise.

Little by little, we can also develop the ability to sustain our Victorious focus during daily work. Whatever we are doing, we can practice doing it more consciously and efficiently, in the state of peace and order. And we can frequently direct our attention within to a particular desire we have and the Victorious state of accomplishment relative to it. This can be done without distracting us from our prescribed task. In the process, we find ourselves more energized and stimulated, and do the task with heightened skills and joy.

Victory is a most powerful energy. Dwelling in it continually can renew an entire personality and build a whole, and truly meaningful life.

As with our work on the other power centers of the Tree, when bringing in the energy streams of Victory it is helpful to remain in a state of *whole consciousness*. This means maintaining a relaxed, unforced awareness of our *whole* selves, all around, throughout, and within our field. This ultimately includes the entire universe of forces and forms in the now.

Let us enter that state of whole consciousness in the present. Become aware of yourself in the now. Gradually feel that awareness expanding, detecting the feelings and vibrations of even the highest and subtlest nature.

Let us remember that we live in a dynamic energy universe. The universe as perceived by our senses is but an abstract, extremely partial, reflection produced by our sensory nervous system in our consciousness. Now sense the whole universe as an infinite, dynamic, energy system in which we live and move and have our being. Realize that there is no such thing as empty space, the forces of light and energy are everywhere present. This is not metaphysics. This is modern physics, and remembering it assists us in our efforts to become wholly aware in the now.

While feeling awareness expanding through your ordered, alert, relaxed state, feel the energy of Victory beginning to stream through. Presently sense the force of Victory related with the ultimate fulfillment of your every desire, in line with your Highest, True, Divine Nature.

This rarely produces a sudden result. The streams of energy begin only subtly to flow through the power center we are working on, in this case, Victory. But the longer we sustain attention there, the more the power center grows and glows.

A truly High and Spiritual life is not a life of repression and inner barrenness. Not according to Qabala. That is false spirituality which curdles the milk of human kindness in a sour hate masquerading as love. The way of Truth and Light is the most fulfilling, inspiring, magnificent way of life. And the way we find such a path is by consciousness of our own inner feelings. As the glow of Victory heats up and intensifies our joy and courage, our faith and fulfillment, we are handling the forces in the present in a healthy, Natural Order, Cosmically True way. This is not the way of bleak sacrifice in hope or belief of some future reward.

It is the way of Victory in the Now, with the signs of approaching even greater dimensions of that indescribably sacred and joyous experience of fulfillment on our path into the Infinite.

SPHERE 8:
GLORY

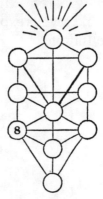

Each moment we can be working on fulfillment through Qabala. With awareness on our goals and the energies and functions of the Spheres on the Tree, we find that we leave the experience of sidereal time. We enter the timeless and eternal now of Harmonic Time.

Intunement to the Qabalistic energies gradually, subtly, unnoticably at first, opens our awareness to eternity. Eternity is charaterized by Harmonic Time. Harmonic Time can be crudely but usefully described as the condition of being wholly at one with our eternal process and our eternal Selves.

Harmonic Time differs from sidereal time in one all important respect. Sidereal time is the concept of time we build by looking at the calendar, our clocks, the apparent movements of the stars in the heavens to **see where we are** relative to where we have been and where we expect to be.

In Harmonic Time we become wholly at one with what *is*, entirely immersed in the adequate handling of the streams of force ever present, actively changing, and requiring constant supervision.

When we fully immerse our consciousness into the now, there is no more sense of time, of past or future. We are too busy working with the True Nature of *what IS*.

Through the practice of dwelling in the forces of Qabala in the present, we gradually awaken to the ever-present flow of the energy currents. This leads to awareness of the sense of purpose, order, wholeness as a guide to our conscious use and direction of the forces represented on the Tree.

This constitutes awakening to our True Self on the force field level. When we make that connection in consciousness, one of the powerful forces received and expressed is represented by the eighth Sphere on the Qabala Tree of Life: Glory.

In the Qabalistic sense, Glory means the condition of being well respected by self and others. There is a level of Truth Consciousness in all beings, though we can live a life of so much repression that we can entirely become unconscious of that level within ourselves. This Truth Consciousness takes us passed the personality's identification with the manifestation of physical sensory phenomenon, into the energy level of vibrational attunement, and through that into the Noetic Light. In other words, Truth Consciousness gradually unfolds into larger dimensions, through transformations. How? One way is by working consciously with the Qabalistic forces in the now.

It is only on the level of Truth Consciousness that a genuine Qabalist or Treader of the Path to the Heights is concerned with Glory. Glory is the energy of feeling good about ourselves. And that is the secret key to others feeling good about us as well.

Glory means Glow-ray. That is, in the sense that when we are feeling good about ourselves, we are really being aware of our True Self. The radiant power of that energy level consciousness then rays forth. We are no longer withdrawn or depressed, but highly expressive, confident and secure within.

Glory is not a power to be toyed with carelessly. Many of us try to fool ourselves into accepting who we are and what we are doing. We convince ourselves as we explain to others how well we are doing and how thoroughly we are meeting any reasonable individual's expectations of what we should be.

Those who talk and boast most of their accomplishments are the least secure. They bring confusion where they go, their own confusion. It is the confusion of word with thing, verbal explanation with actual energy fact.

We can only **DISCOVER** what makes us feel truly good about ourselves. We cannot impose it. We can sense when we are doing something poorly, not fulfilling our responsibility, taking wrong short-cuts.

There is a safeguard from self-deception. It is **SELF-AWARENESS**. Right now, become self-aware. Observe your present state. Sense your feelings while remaining aware of your environment. Now, in that conscious state, relax, breath a long, full breath, feel the experience of Glory entering your field. Sense good feelings about yourself in the present.

This is not a mental exercise, it is a conscious *feeling* exercise. As soon as we begin this, the first thing we often find is a feeling of the opposite nature. It feels funny to try to feel good about ourselves. It feels vain or narcisstic - and that is a good and healthy sign.

Do not ignore such a sign. When we are feeling wrong it usually means we are actually doing something wrong. Many of us try to block wrong feelings because we fear it will make us hesitate and lose our confidence. Blocking feelings only makes us lose touch with Truth.

When feelings of being untrue to your higher, whole, balanced Self are aroused, go to work on the energies. So maneuver your state that you find the way to relax, and in peace feel good about yourself in a truly good, wholesome, balanced and harmonious way.

Our feelings of pain, even on the inner levels, guide us into the True Light of our Self.

It is the wholly self-honest and aware state of feeling good about ourselves in the now that is represented by Glory on the Tree of Life.

This is a state to be practiced. It is a healthy, inspiring state of faith in ourselves that brings out our highest potential, peace and joy.

It is often helpful to take a piece of time, say, ten minutes, and devote it to the conscious cultivation of one of the powers of the Tree. For example, take the next ten minutes, try to stay as continually aware as you can of the Glorious state. The attention drifts many times during the early phases of our practice of this nature. But gradually the muscle of control is strengthened, our will awakened, and we can sustain our focus longer and longer. The longer conscious awareness is filled with the force of Glory, the more powerfully does it flow and work on our behalf.

The reader will notice that, on the Tree of Life, Glory and Victory are on the same level. This gives us an indication of their intimate relationship.

The easiest way to discover Glory is by dwelling consciously in Victory until we find it. For example, right now, bring to mind a particular goal, desire, or future accomplishment that is important to you. The key to Glory is **FUTURE,** because by looking at our past accomplishment for feelings of pride we actually lose touch with our True Selves in the **NOW** and what our **PRESENT** job, purpose, or structure, function, order is.

With your goal in mind, begin to feel the sense of Victory in association with its accomplishment. In that state, you can now find the feeling of Glory. When we feel our fulfillment we radiate self-respect, and others begin to respect us more.

This is something anyone can prove for himself. It is a very powerful, though subtle mechanism.

It is when we are feeling deprived or denied of an important, deeply desired experience or accomplishment, that we become withdrawn, shy, disrespectful of ourselves. Others then unconsciously register and respond to those vibrations, and show disrespect to us as well. This makes us look worse, make clumsy errors, and the frustration in our life builds and builds.

The solution is the Glorious radiance we contact in conscious Victory.

Let us apply it again, this time to a relationship. Become aware of a particular kind of relationship you want in your life, a whole, balanced, fulfilling relationship. With that in mind, feel the sense of Victory which accompanies the feeling of its manifestation in your life. Feel as though you now have all that you have ever or could ever want in a relationship to the deepest and highest levels of fulfillment.

Keeping that state, that energy in consciousness, begin to feel that whole and balanced self-respect which can only come by fulfilling one's Self in Truth. It is the feeling that we have and deserve all that is Good and True and Beautiful. The feeling of deserved fulfillment.

The way into Glory is the feeling of fulfillment with the sense of being worthy of it to the nth or limitless degree. We can all feel that now if we relax and become aware of those vibrations, those energy currents circulating within our conscious field.

Glory, then, is the state of feeling True to our Selves. Feel that now. Become aware of your present state, what you are feeling or subtly expressing in your vibratory radiations. And gently intune the consciousness to the True Self you are, the condition of being harmoniously expressive in Truth.

Glory is a wonderful, nourishing feeling. It really feeds us with the power to achieve and become all that we can **BE**.

How many times have we felt embarrassed by others? How much pain of shame, and guilt, and sense of inferiority and inadequacy have we felt because of how **OTHERS** seemed to treat or feel about us? **MUCH TOO MUCH.**

As we work on Glory we free ourselves from that type of suffering. Imagine, we never have to feel deprived and second rate again! That is because we are working on feeling Glory, true at-one-ment with the fulfillment of our True Self.

One of the magical aspects of this work on Glory is its affects upon others. As we outgrow the weak tendency to feel bad about ourselves, others will find it more and more difficult to feel that way about us. This is not some occult means of manipulating others. It is simply a natural fact. The better we feel about ourselves, without repression, the more highly regarded and respected we become by others.

However, there will always be those who will never show us any respect. They are afraid to because they do not know how to respect others without losing respect for themselves. Especially macho men seem to have this difficulty in their relationships with women. When our own self-respect is insecure, it is far more difficult to respect others.

Respecting others in the right way can be real blessing for both of us. To respect someone in the right way means to be aware of **THEIR** True Self within. It is not assuming the role of petty, placating, superficial flatterer feeling like dirt in another's presence. That is not real.

Let us see if we can do that now. Become aware of someone important to you in your life, or an ideal someone whom you would like to have in your life. With that other in mind, begin to sense that one's True Self, True Structure, Function, Order in Cosmos in the now. It begins as a vague sort of subtle sensing, non-descript vibrations or energy currents stimulating our inner being most tenuously.

With that one's True Self vibration in consciousness, begin to tune into Glory. Begin to feel yourself fulfilling your deepest desires and needs, and being worthy of it, deserving of it, possessing the talents and the gifts to earn and fairly bring it about.

Now, firmly based in Glory yourself, you can help another into that illuminous, radiant field. Become aware of the vibrations, of the state of, harmony with the True Self of that other.

True Glory takes place on the Individualizing level, not the personality level. No one is any better or worse than anyone else. To the degree that one is in harmony with their own True Self and the True Self of others, that one knows True Glory. He or she will find the help and attention of those who Know and are aware.

As we feel the sense of Divinity, the vibrations of the Cosmic Individualizing process taking place in another, we must remain very aware of ourselves. Only in awareness of ourselves can we avoid the easy error of personalizing the powerful energy currents of another's field.

In that conscious state, then feel the sense of what attitude that Individual Truly needs to help fulfill his or her own highest potential. To personalize it would mean subjugating ourselves, flattering them, puffing them up with false pride. We keep it on the True, Individualizing level by sensing what attitude they need from us while we remain in our balanced, conscious, ordered state of strength.

NEVER allow another to be so demanding of so-called praise and respect that it knocks you off your balance. The Qabala Tree of Life shows three rows of up-and-down running Spheres. These are called Pillars. And three Pillars symbolizes **BALANCE, STABILITY,** and **STRENGTH.**

Enter that state of balance, stability, and inner strength now so that we know what is being described here. Feel inner peace, stability, steadiness and power within you and throughout you, subtly flowing and gradually increasing.

In that whole and balanced state, we can enter Glory without fooling ourselves or confusing others. And in that state we can progress into our own Highest Potential, while aiding others to do the same.

In so doing, we slowly enter the Timeless State of the Eternal Now, working in Harmonic Time on the True Self Processes we **ARE.**

SPHERE 9:
FOUNDATION

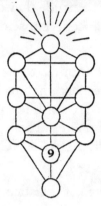

There is an interesting correlation between the Qabala and ancient Oriental Wisdom dating back to earlier than five-thousand years B.C. The Upanishads is a body of spiritual writings of ancient India. These writings are the oldest known. Their language is Sanskrit, the most ancient as well.

Upanishad is a Sanskrit word meaning, basically, to sit and listen to One Who Knows. This is similar to the meaning of Qabala, a Hebrew word, meaning Oral Teaching or "from mouth to ear".

The teachings of the Upanishads, which embody the Spiritual Wisdom of India and represent the highest levels of Perception of the most advanced Sages and Seers, is completely in line with the Qabala. The orientation to the Quest for Truth, Self-Mastery, and Victory for the Higher Self are all in keeping with the teachings expressed in the Yoga Sutras of Patangali, the Bhagavad Gita, and the other Upanishads.

Does this mean that there is one central stream of Wisdom, of Truth, a stream which survives to guide us to this day? All evidence seems to indicate that.

Another point worthy of note is the Bhagavad Gita's reference to a Sacred Tree Of Life which holds the key to our freedom from bondage to the lower self. Is the Qabala Tree of Life what is being referred to in that aged script? For all intents and purposes, it may as well be, for living in the energies of Qabala's Tree results in that inner liberation.

This brings us to Sphere nine of the Tree, Foundation. In some ways this is the most essential level to master ourselves on.

The Foundation is strength, endurance, poise. The reader will notice this Sphere sits upon the Middle Pillar of the Tree, representing its correlation to balance, centeredness, and equipoise.

The energy, state and function represented by this Sphere is highly healing and stabilizing. Let us feel it now. Begin by emptying your lungs of air as completely as you can. Slowly and gently exhale.

When you can breathe out no further, begin breathing in slowly and gently. As you do, feel the calming, patient, stable forces of the Foundation drawing into you through your breath. Feel the peace and power of endurance which is the Foundation flowing throughout you.

Now sense yourself being strong enough to withstand any challenge or difficulty that life may confront you with, in a poised and easy fashion. This is the **ESSENCE** of Inner Freedom; the **FOUNDATION** of all further controlling of our forces.

The Foundation level is so important because it gives us the energy to sustain ourselves, to survive and endure any plight or obstacle. As we practice maintaining our peace and poise - **TRUE INNER POISE** - during daily living, life becomes easier. We gradually waste less and less of our energy on fear, worry, stress, or anxiety. And we can then use that energy to experience Higher States of Perception, to function ever more Wisely and productively, to bring about what we want in life.

Feel that flow of **THE POWER TO ENDURE IN PEACE** right now. This is a helpful state to tune into before entering an important business meeting or facing that difficult phone call.

The longer we remain conscious of the Foundation energy in us, the deeper our peace and strength expands. In time, we can develop the poise to handle virtually any duty or experience deemed necessary with ease, composure, and a healthy sense of humor. This is gradually attained through the steady practice of living in the Foundation **CONSCIOUSLY.**

The Foundation is the base upon which all higher structures are built. Without a good Foundation, a house is weak and vulnerable.

Our Victories, Beauty, Wisdom, and Noetic Perception are all attainments requiring good, solid Foundations. Every project must have one; every business, relationship, or home.

We develop a good strong Foundation relative to any enterprise by enduring opposition and resistance intelligently.

Every endeavor meets with a degree of resistance to its accomplishment. The higher the dream, the more Severe the changes we strive to make, the more opposition we must confront in the process. That is Natural Order. Just look at Nature. A flower grows quickly and dies quickly. A tree grows much more slowly, and much larger, requiring the slow developments of good, strong roots and a sturdy trunk.

Resistance and opposition to a project is actually a good sign. It means that what we are attempting is probably of very high value compared to what presently is happening. It means our goal is truly worthy.

For example, when we try to live a life that will fulfill our True Self in line with other True Selves, we are attempting quite a bit. The resistance to such a life-path is always strong. In some ways it is far easier to live a life of unconsciousness and superficiality. It is far easier to become confused than to master our minds and see things clearly and constructively.

But hard work pays off. It only *seems* easier to take the easy road. But the results are as weak as the effort.

By consciously working on the Foundation phase of an operation or project, we can actually deepen the stability and heighten the attainments of our success.

Let us see what it means to work consciously on the Foundation level for positive results. Select a goal of yours in life. When you have it in mind, become aware of its highest and most satisfying degree of attainment. For example, if you have a particular career goal, begin to sense how it would feel if your absolute ideal career manifested for you, if you had it now.

With that goal's attainment in mind, begin to feel peace, stability, self-control within. Look for and free yourself from any sense of stress, impatience, or insecurity. Just be aware of your goal in the state of calm and peaceful inner strength.

This is conscious work on the Foundation. In that poise, work on your dreams. And when you hit a snag, when it seems like you might be working in vain, let go of your goal and just retreat back to your Foundation.

In the Foundation we feel peace and strength, calm and order. Begin feeling that now and you enter your Foundation.

When all else fails, do not fail yourself. That is really the axiom of the Foundation .

To fail ourselves means to lose self-control, to feel,

say, think, and do things that are not helpful, only hurtful.

Essentially, the Foundation of our lives is our **SELF-CONTROL**. Whatever the goal, no matter how high or far we must travel or progress to attain it, **SELF-CONTROL IS THE KEY.**

Self-Control means peace and calm when things are going against us, when distractions arise, when people are not cooperating. We can actually use oppositions like these as opportunities to grow and strengthen our progress.

The next time it seems that things are going against you, take a deep breath and enter the Foundation. In the state of calm self-control, allow your forces to replenish, or continue to direct them in efforts to bring about what you want.

The more poised and centered we can remain as we work for what we want, the more strongly connected to that goal we become. In time, we will attain.

Whatever brings about results is the base or Foundation of those results. Every so-called "thing" or "object" that exists is actually a *process*. A process is an ordered sequence of changes, a chain of reactions or results. Even a piece of wood, which appears solid and static to our five physical senses, is actually a dynamic configuration of energy units, an ever changing *process* on the sub-microscopic level. The Foundation of the piece of wood, or any so-called "solid object" is the series of phases or activities resulting in its present state in the *now*.

The same holds true for a relationship with the type of individual you want to have a relationship with. To work on the Foundation level is to do what you can do in line with its coming about. If it is not here yet in the way you want it, that simply means that more work is needed on the Foundation or *preparatory* level.

All creative processes are shaky in the early phases. A marriage, a business, a higher state of consciousness all demonstrate this law. Disorganization, internal weakness, and attracting difficulties and opposition are things we must pass through if our efforts are to reap rewards.

It is the calm and patient handling of these early phases that builds the Foundation for future rewards. We often want to just give up in disgust when crises pile up. It is at these times that we return to the Foundation mode of functioning to endure. In time, the cycle of opposition will pass. If we have endured, we can then progress.

Select another goal or aspiration you have. When you know what that is, consider one major difficulty or opposition that you have to contend with in order to achieve it.

When you have that opposition in mind, enter the Foundation. Feel peace and calm patience. Feel poise, persistence, and deep inner peace.

We often feel a sense of the obstacle just disintegrating when we enter that state. And it actually begins to do that. By going into peace, we are actually taking the energy from the obstacle and absorbing it into our own inner strength.

We usually become very impatient when it comes to opposition, non-cooperation, and other forms of resistance to our desires. We tend to want to get them over with as soon as we can. As a Wise One has said: "Everybody wants to go faster than God."

Impatience, frustration, resisting the difficulties is exactly the **OPPOSITE** of intelligently responding to what *is*. That only aggravates the situation, makes it worse.

Entering the Foundation, cooling it and accepting what *is* strengthens the ordering forces of the situation.

Sometimes, we go through a situation that is difficult, and we are tempted to seek another's aid. This may be for a financial or even a spiritual purpose. There is certainly nothing wrong with seeking help from others. In fact, according to Qabala, until one finds a True Wisdom Teacher, One Who Knows The Process, one cannot make the final crossing into the Noetic Light.

However, in this, as in all else, timing is crucial. Sometimes, it is best **NOT** to ask for assistance, but to struggle to make it on our own. In that way, "our own" is pushed to new heights. This is something to remember in business matters. The solution to a crisis is not necessarily to take out another loan, but to squeak through using our **INNER** resources, our skills, ingenuity, and courage. Whatever we rely upon grows stronger.

The important point to remember is that the Foundation is a consciousness we can enter. Feel it now. Just sense the ray of peace, strength, and order permeating your inner state.

It is in that state that we can endure all conflict, free ourselves from the uncontrol which results in painful, unconstructive thought, feeling, speech, or action.

In the Foundation we can wait, and work patiently, along the Way to our Oneness with our Higher Self.

The lower self is another name for the personality level. This is the level of our personal attachments, demands, desires, and expectations.

But there is a Higher, a Truer Self. This is the level of our Individualizing Structure, Function, Order. By practicing the Foundation, we make way for the vibrations of that Structure, Function, Order of our True Self to permeate our field of consciousness, and guide us into identity with our Divine Natures.

The Foundation level is the state of stillness; stillness

practiced in the face of opposition and opportunity; the stillness of stability, clear awareness, and peace.

As we practice this amid all the experiences of daily living, the Foundation of our emergence into a higher and truer state of consciousness is established.

SPHERE 10:
THE KINGDOM

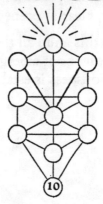

Qabala teaches us that part of living an Enlightened, worthwhile life is taking care of earthly demands. There is nothing unspiritual about our worldly necessities, comforts, and technologies.

In fact, the needs of the material plane must be met in order to serve the True Purpose of our lives. The lessons we learn about the Laws of Cosmos, and the skills and powers we develop in the process, result in our growth as Cosmic Beings. That growth or continuing evolvement is the essential Purpose of our lives.

Beyond that, we each have a Cosmic Job to do in this life. The performance of that Cosmic Service requires a healthy, balanced state of being. We cannot continue to serve, Grow, and Learn our Lessons, if we are hungry, ill, exhausted, or disorganized.

Society changes with the times. The needs for modern, city dwelling man include stream-lined, fuel efficient autos, leisure time to unwind in the far-away forests, books and classes for higher education, a credit card to rent a car, etc. We need "acceptable" attire, our children have desires carefully nurtured by shrewd, manipulative, high-tech advertising.

To put it all bluntly, life today is expensive. It requires abundant resources and that never comes without much hard work. For those who seem fortunate enough to have material resources handed to them "on a silver platter", it still has to be spent and managed well, expressive of the True or Higher Self, if peace and happiness are to be found.

Money is not "the root of all evil". As long as they are sought and handled for the growth and expansion of our ability to tune into, express and identify with our True and Higher Self, material resources are a blessing and not a curse. Far from being "evil", they are, to that extent, our Cosmic and Divine responsibility to manage and accrue.

We now find ourselves at the tenth and final Sphere of the Qabala Tree of Life. This is named The Kingdom. It is concerned with the Manifestation and completion of a given force, form, or function. The Kingdom is the material plane.

Let us see how this Sphere applies to our own growth and Fulfillment. According to Qabala, our purpose is to become Light Beings. This means our consciousness transfigured into the perfect expression of Divine Light. To apply the Kingdom to that purpose means to work on the Manifestation, Materialization, or Completion of that process.

Right now, let us *experience* that high goal within us. Feel, become *aware of* what it would be like, what it IS like to actually complete that process and manifest that transfiguration completely.

Working on The Kingdom means working on the **FINAL PHASE** of an operation.

We can separate any process or endeavor into three basic phases. These are the beginning, the middle, and the end. The Kingdom represents the ending or completion stage of any project.

According to Qabala, our physical or worldly situation is the final stage of the Manifestation Process.

Our financial situation, our job, home, relationships, health, possessions, environments, etc. are all **RESULTS** of **WHAT WE DO**. In that sense, these are part of The Kingdom. The Kingdom is not just the completion of a process, but the manifestation of our Worldly Life.

The fact is, worldly and physical conditions represent the last stage or **FINAL AFFECTS** of any given force. That is why The Kingdom and the Earth-plane are one.

This level is connected to the rest of the Tree. Our Worldly Life needs to be structurally aligned with and suited to the fulfillment of the other functions represented by the Spheres of Qabala. And to fulfill those functions completely produces that Worldly and Physical harmony and order.

Let us see how The Kingdom applies to our financial or material stability, security, comfort and independence. Become aware now of the final stages of that state in your own life. Work on feeling the physiological and worldly manifestation and experience of that process. Observe the change or state of your emotions and feeling-mood-attitude which accompanies that fulfillment, that completion of the process.

The longer we dwell consciously in that Kingdom level, the more energy we direct into it, and the more deeply conscious of it we become.

Our worldly or Kingdom needs go beyond having resources. They include working at a satisfying job or career. Right now, let us feel ourselves experiencing the final, manifest stage of that process. Sense its physical manifestation, its having been accomplished.

During this practice, sometimes a kind of light flashes in our consciousness, around the area of our forehead, in which we can, in some whole, complete, and intuitive fashion, actually see and experience this world in which we are already fulfilled in that area. When one experiences in that light one has truly entered the dimension in cosmos of The Kingdom, in the Light, which is actually patterned as the Qabala Tree. Some call this mere mysticism. Others, including this author, know that it is real.

We live in a dynamic energy universe in which all that exists is actually forces. And all forces have their completion in the Kingdom. For example, there is The Kingdom of emotions. The kingdom of an emotion or feeling is its final stage, where it is completely manifest and has produced its physiological and worldly results.

Let us work on The Kingdom of inner peace. Begin to feel and sense inner peace flowing within you. Now, become aware of the state of your complete manifestation of that state. Feel it in every inch of your being, substantive and complete. Sense its ordering and harmonizing affects and reflection in your worldly and physical life. Be aware of yourself fully in that manifest, physical world where your inner peace is in all that exists.

Only by working on The Kingdom of the fulfillment of a given desire can we complete our satisfaction. Until The Kingdom of fulfillment has been reached, the process is not finished, loose ends are dangling free.

Here is how we work on the Kingdom level of the fulfillment of a given desire. Become aware right now of a particular desire that you have. Begin to sense what it feels like to have that desire completely fulfilled. Become aware of the energies of its manifestation, the physiological presence of it in your cells, your worldly environments and situations.

To be aware of the Kingdom Level of a particular fulfillment means to sense its presence in all that exists, and then to sense its manifestation, expression and reflection in all that exists. Experience that fulfillment's re-structuring affects on all that physically IS.

In this universe, everything affects everything.

Nothing and no one is separate or alone. The ancients symbolized this fact by drawing a serpent with its tail in its mouth. Albert Einstein described it in his theory of relativity far more elaborately. We work on The Kingdom when we *tune into* the "mouth full of tail" at the Serpent's head. In other words, by consciously realizing and experiencing the end results of the chain of affects set into motion by a given force or condition.

Working in The Kingdom state of consciousness of a given fulfillment magnetically pulls or draws the lines of force of our life's energy field into the pattern we desire. *This has a measurable affect upon the physical and psychic (psychological) conditions of our situation in line with our True Fulfillment.*

Working on The Kingdom level includes the actual visible, physical levels of labor. This means physically waking up in the morning, arriving at work on time, lifting our heavy loads, making our tough decisions, ringing up the sales, putting in our time, etc. All of this "physical" level, however, represents the *final* results of the process which led up to its manifestation.

Sometimes we cannot work on a given project on that "macroscopic" (apparent to the five physical senses) level. For example, a worker who finds himself laid off cannot go to the office that day. A lover who lost her mate cannot take him in her arms and actually tell him how she feels.

Many of us are completely identified with the "macroscopic" level as being the only reality. We do not realize that actually having a job or relationship we want is just the final phase of a creative process.

Not having what we want on the level that we want it leaves us with no time or energy to waste on fear, complaining, or dissatisfaction. Our time and energy need to be focused on the **MANIFESTATION PROCESS.**

Work on the **MANIFESTATION PROCESS** means working with **ALL TEN SPHERES** of the Qabala Tree of Life relative to our particular, conscious need or goal.

Perhaps there is something or a particular situation that you presently have which you are happy with and want to keep. It could be a relationship with someone, a new car, or a heightened state of consciousness. Well, as much as you may want to keep things as they are, it is still **IMPOSSIBLE.** Nothing stays the same. Everything and everyone and every situation is constantly changing on the sub-microscopic levels. Sooner or later that changing process will become apparent. That is one of the Cosmic, Natural Order Laws governing The Kingdom.

However, growth is the solution. Take, for example, a relationship with someone dear to you. It will not and cannot remain as it is, no matter how badly you or I may want it to. Things will change, individuals change, and relationships must change with them. To depend upon blind hope or expectation that things **WILL** or **MIGHT** continue as they are, guarantees they will only deteriorate and degenerate. But by working on the cultivation, development, and improvement of that relationship, by working on keeping in touch with and keeping up with the changing, growing needs of the relationship's continued harmony, we direct our Kingdom's progress. The manifestation we dearly love then evolves along with us, as does our love for it, in this ever-changing and evolving dynamic energy universe.

Relative to this there is a healthy and worthwhile practice. It is in making note of the situations we have that we want to continue. We often spend so much time and attention looking at what we are dissatisfied with, we fail to appreciate adequately all that is good in our lives.

When we see what we like and want to continue, it is time to evaluate our situation, look for the changes already taking place. Look for any circumstances that seem to be moving in on what you want to keep.

When we see what is affecting a situation, we can begin to adapt and make the necessary adjustments to **TAKE ADVANTAGE** of what is happening. As was pointed out in the previous chapter, on the Foundation, we can often use opposition to strengthen ourselves, a relationship, a business, or other processes by calmly enduring the onslaught.

The sooner we see what is happening in our Kingdom, the more effectively and easily can we respond, adapt, prepare, and adjust for it.

The Kingdom, then, represents the final phase of any operation, the earthly or material plane of a given project, function, force, or relationship.

As we focus our attention and efforts on the completion, the materialized fulfillment of a given want or need, we are bringing into manifestation The Kingdom of our True Fulfillment which already exists in Light's Regions.

Let us end this chapter with a strictly Qabalistic exercise. This is the exercise of applying the Kingdom to the states and powers represented by the Spheres on the Tree of Life.

The first Sphere is The Crown. This represents the highest level of Perception, Noetic Awareness on the Mind Level. Truth Consciousness. Feel and sense that Awareness permeating your being and your life, being completely manifest and materialized in your world, your cosmos. This is the Kingdom of your Crown.

The second Sphere is Wisdom. Wisdom means doing that which helps in a situation, on every level of our being. It means useful, conscious functioning. Feel the sense now of perfectly and infinitely embodying that state. Become aware of every facet of yourself and your physical life expressing your fulfillment of that state. This is The Kingdom of your Wisdom.

The third Sphere is Understanding. This means insight or seeing into what is happening, seeing and Knowing what to do about what *is*. Feel that state manifesting throughout your entire being. Be aware of your life being the perfect reflection and embodiment of your mastery on that level. This is The Kingdom of your Understanding.

Mercy is the fourth Sphere on the Tree. This is the sphere of ease, gentleness, and pleasure. Completely be aware of yourself perfectly balanced and masterful in the use of this force in your life and relationships. Be aware of the total peace, harmony and freedom of abundance it brings to your physical, emotional, and every other level of your life. This is the Kingdom of your Mercy.

The fifth Sphere is named Severity. This Sphere represents the doing of what needs to be done for the accomplishment of what we have chosen. It is the non-reactive, step-by-step, methodical and systematic approach to the handling of any given situation. Feel that state, that ability and approach in you now. Feel it changing the cells in your body, flowing through you in right measure for your mastery and peace. Be fully aware of yourself and your life as both are changed, affected, and completed by that calm, successful functioning. This is The Kingdom of your Severity.

Beauty is the next Sphere, numbered six. This is our consciousness of harmony and order, inspiration and satisfaction. Feel that force in your being, flowing. Sense yourself entering harmony with what *is* in your present moment. Realize the limitless materialization of your Beauty in all that is, formed and created by that High energy pattern. This is The Kingdom of your Beauty.

Next comes the seventh Sphere, Victory. This is the feeling of accomplishment or triumph accompanying the achievement of a goal, the fulfillment of a real desire. Feel the sense of your triumph permeating your being and changing your cells. Feel it in the air you inhale and exhale. Be aware of your whole life, world, and cosmos being charged, changed, and completely manifesting your utterly triumphant joy and light. This is The Kingdom of your Victory.

Glory follows Victory and is numbered eight on the Tree. Glory is the awareness of ourselves as being the fulfilled and Victorious one. Feel that Glory in your flesh and bones, your hair and teeth. Sense its affect upon all the universe, every part and level of it. See it being rayed back at you from everything in your environment and every star in the heavens. This is The Kingdom of your Glory.

And the Foundation is the ninth Sphere. This is our strength and capacity to endure. It is our stability and True Equipoise. Be aware of this state fully manifested in the structure of your limbs, in every physical article, in the True Substance of all that is, which is the energy field generated by **CONSCIOUS LIGHT**. This is The Kingdom of your Foundation.

And finally we come to The Kingdom of The Kingdom. In other words, we arrive at the complete cosmic and worldly manifestation of our Heavenly Kingdom which already exists and waits for us to "bring it down to earth". We do this by entering that Kingdom in Heavenly Light while remaining firmly grounded, aware in the present, aware of The Kingdom as it presently is on earth as well. In that way we become the **BRIDGE.**

Qabala has shown us the Cosmic Blueprint of The Kingdom of Heaven. And our purpose is to be the Conscious Bridge or Conscious Co-creator. That is why you were born, to do your part. And so was I.

May we do our Cosmic Parts well, and thus know the True Peace Which Passeth All Understanding, **TOGETHER.**

PART II

APPLICATIONS
OF THE SYSTEM
AS A WHOLE

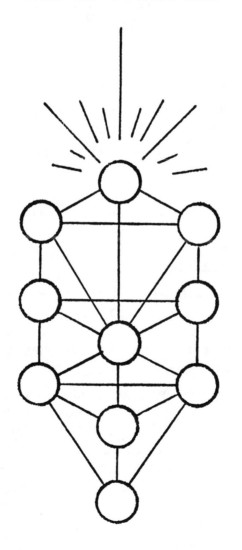

INNER FREEDOM THROUGH QABALA

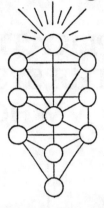

Beyond presenting an explanation of how the forces, states of consciousness, and functions represented by the Qabala Tree of Life can be used by us for our benefit, the aim of this book has been to guide the reader through the actual exercise of those forces, states, and functional patterns of behavior.

To the degree that one can actually exercise these **AT WILL**, that one has *Inner Freedom*. The more one practices these, the more powerful and expansive that Inner Freedom becomes.

The value of Inner Freedom is that it provides us with the ability to maintain self-control for more harmonious, constructive, joyous daily living. Inner Freedom means the power to control one's state, activity, and reactivity on all levels of one's self.

For ages, mankind has tried to find happiness within by changing the world which seems to be "outside" of self. This has not worked. The result is the overpopulation, ecological deterioration, social decadence, and nuclear proliferation of our day. Mankind, after all of this "outer" manipulation, is perhaps more unhappy, agnostic, and frustrated than ever before.

Throughout these same ages, however, relatively

small numbers of individuals and groups have preserved, revered, and passed on a different approach. It is the Inner Way. The system of Qabala represents one of those approaches to happiness.

It has been proven over and over, and each reader can prove it for himself and herself, that we control our circumstances and destinies when we control ourselves. In fact, it can be validly asserted that the so-called "outer" is but a reflection of the state and functional conditions of the "inner".

Let us be more specific, and look at how each Sphere on the Tree represents a force, a state, and a function.

The Crown represents Perception, Conscious Awareness of what **IS**. Enter that state now to the best of your present ability. Direct awareness into what **IS**. Become conscious of the experience of seeing into the True Nature of what is happening in the now, both within yourself and in your here-now environment.

The Crown represents a **FORCE** in that entering Perception changes the situation. It begins to bring order into it, a peace, clarity, and order you can soon feel. That force field actually radiates, influencing the here-now, and our future, attracting and manifesting more insight, order, and happiness in our lives and in those with whom we come in contact.

The Crown represents a **STATE** of consciousness because Perceptive Awareness is an experience we can feel. As we work innerly on entering this state, all other states are modified by it. For instance, if we are sad, working on entering deeper and deeper into Perception of what is going on begins to permeate us with peace, gradually dissipating the gloom.

And The Crown represents a **FUNCTION** in that entering Perception, and attending to the daily tasks in that state, changes the way we do things. It forces us to live more slowly, noticing more, assimilating the data, looking at where we are and responding more consciously in the **NOW**.

It takes a certain degree of Inner Freedom to direct our state, forces, and functioning into the Perceptive mode. But the more we practice, the more ability we develop to do that. In time, our power to apply The Crown becomes so immense, that we can perceive the happy, harmonious, deeply meaningful way to respond to any event. One at this level is labeled "Master of Life".

The second Sphere, named Wisdom, represents consciously controlled activity. Enter Wisdom now. Become aware of yourself. Notice your present state, feelings, sensings, activity. Do not label or think about what you are doing. Just observe and consciously experience in the **NOW**. At the same time, direct yourself. Become aware of what you want in life, in the **NOW**, and direct and control yourself accordingly.

Wisdom is a **FORCE** in that it represents the force of intelligent self-control. Being Wise is to exert a natural, harmonious pressure to keep our inner and outer activities aligned with our highest and truest wants and needs. In the Natural Order, our forces will not automatically take care of us or flow in an ordered pattern. We must watch, control, and direct ourselves, our states in the now. This is Wisdom, the continuous alignment of our forces with our True Self. Doing this to the best of our ability generates a deep ordering pattern into the events and circumstances of our lives. That is the **FORCE** of Wisdom *applied.*

Wisdom is a **STATE** of consciousness because, like The Crown (Perception), it is an experience we can detect, recognize, and observe happening to us. Enter Wisdom and notice how your **STATE** is affected. Stay in it for a while and notice the affects it seems to produce on your relationships, how it seems to attract opportunities and bring you into more balanced and harmonious environments.

Wisdom is a way of **FUNCTIONING** as well because it is the integration of awareness, intelligence, and control into activity. To be Wise is to do that which pays, to measure and observe what we are doing, and how we are affecting our situation. It means being aware of our goals, needs, objectives and keeping our activities in line with bringing about our conscious fulfillment in the most efficient, compassionate manner.

The third Sphere, Understanding, represents awareness or insight into how something works. Feel yourself entering the experience of Understanding now. Sense Understanding of what is going on in your life unfolding deep in your consciousness. The longer you remain in this state, entering it ever more deeply, the more lucid and comprehensive will your insight and awareness develop.

Understanding is a **FORCE** in that, like the previous two, entering it, working on it, begins to influence any set of circumstances in the direction of order, enlightenment, and fulfillment.

Understanding is a **STATE** in that it is an experience you can feel. Entering it affects our experience of being, our condition on all levels. Stop intentionally applying Understanding for a moment, and then re-enter it. You will notice how differently it feels to be dwelling in its matrix of forces.

And Understanding is a **FUNCTION or WAY OF FUNCTIONING**. Raise your arms up and down while dwelling in its state and forces. Notice how it subtly affects what you are doing within when you raise and lower your arms in and out of that state. While raising and lowering your arms, work your consciousness into Understanding exactly what you are doing it for and how best to do it for the good of the whole.

Mercy represents ease, leisure, pleasure. Enter the experience of those energies in the now. Begin to feel them flowing through your being.

Mercy is a **FORCE**. When you allow it to flow through your being it begins to manifest abundance, joyous circumstances, and all that you appreciate and desire. When we take it easy on ourselves, we give the universe a message to take it easy on us, to hug and kiss us with her bliss. A force is anything that produces affects, and mercy produces the affects of increasing the flow of whatever we allow into our lives.

The **STATE** of Mercy is plain to see. Right now, simply feel happy, pleasant, gentle and easy. That state radiates out and fills the space and relationships we enter and dwell in as well.

Mercy affects our **WAY OF FUNCTIONING** by lightening our footsteps, slowing us down, tuning us to the expression and appreciation of humor and generosity in our daily living patterns.

Severity, the fifth Sphere on the Tree of Life, represents force, Justice, doing that which must be done. It is cool, calculating, systematic, and necessary limitation. It is discipline, control, restraint. Enter Severity now, without losing your balance in Mercy. Consciously, gently, apply consciousness, measure, control, and discipline to yourself in the now.

Severity is the **FORCE** which protects us from excessive leniency, impracticality, or the overstepping of healthy and compassionate limitations. When practiced, it releases a force of protection as well as attracting that which is important to us.

It is a **STATE** you can feel most clearly right after entering the state of Mercy. Severity preserves the managable and harmonious state of simplicity in ourselves, our environments, and our affairs.

The **WAY OF FUNCTIONING** which is Severity is the cool, methodical, no-nonsense way. When applied, it enables us to penetrate through the most complex of circumstances in cool ease. Practice Severity while walking across your room, and notice how your steps become more measured and sure, your posture more confident and erect, your vision keen and focused.

Beauty is the transcendent joy we experience when our love nature is fully aroused. Enter that state now. Experience the feelings of Beauty you contact when triggered by the most appealing sights, sounds, feels, or moments. Recall the state when just the right piece of music is played or the highest dream comes true.

The **FORCE** of Beauty is demonstrated by the upliftment we feel under its influence. And the more it is experienced, the more it begins to manifest in our forms, faculties, and environments. We begin to attract more and more of the manifestations which express our Beauty and reflect if back into us.

Beauty is a **STATE** of consciousness. It is a feeling, an inner experience that radiates out and fills those with whom we are present in mind or vicinity.

The way that Beauty affects our **FUNCTIONING** is to guide our hands and minds in the creation of that which reflects more charm and creative power. Whether we are working on a machine or a relationship with another human, living in Beauty helps us to make the thing shine in its own inspirational way. That shine sparkles in the eyes of those who view our works, eliciting their special favor in return.

Victory, on the Qabala Tree of Life, represents staying wholly focused on bringing about what you want. Become aware of something you want in your life right now, something meaningful or important to you. Keeping that in mind, become aware of the overall experience of your fulfillment in that area. If it is a particular job you want, be aware right now of the overall experience of having it, working in it, enjoying it, **BEING THERE** in peace, balance, fullness and light.

The **FORCE** of Victory is to drive us through whatever obstacles or resistance might be in our way, to ultimately bring success to us and us into success.

The **STATE** of consciousness represented by Victory is most obvious. When practiced, we are actually living in fulfillment. We live in the experience manufactured by consciousness and will.

Victory affects our **FUNCTIONING** by keeping us working on and in what we want to accomplish. We may be working on subtle, inner levels or more apparent "external" levels, but Victory keeps us focused.

Glory is the experience of self-worth we experience when Victory is our state. As long as we are focused on the Victorious condition, self-respect radiates from our True inner Self in a pure, non-egotistical way. It is not the sense of superiority to others. Glory is the feeling and power of being True to your Higher Self, your own divine nature, whose purpose it is to be compassionate, aware, and in harmony with others.

Enter the **FORCE** of that non-egotistical Self-fulfillment, and it radiates forth. Others begin to sense that special quality which is Truly You, and respond with helpfulness and love.

The **STATE** of Glory is that feeling and light that we enter in our consciousness, in which we actually see ourselves with stature. Right now, relax, feel completely balanced and unemotional. Then, calmly sense yourself worthwhile, capable, trustworthy. It cannot be stressed enough how important it is to remain impersonal about

Glory to keep it from degenerating into false egotism and vainglory.

Glory changes our **FUNCTIONING**. Anyone who has had a serious bout with feeling low self-worth has observed the self-destructive acts and negativism it breeds. Living in Glory is just as powerful, but gives birth to healthy, helpful, constructive acts. This in turn, attracts circumstances ever more in harmony with one's highest states of being.

The ninth Sphere on the Tree, Foundation, represents stability, strength, and endurance. It represents patience, persistence, and a base of order and union. Enter the Foundation now. Feel peace, order, and stable union with that which is Good, True and Beautiful in your life. Foundation is the non-rushed peace and poise which resides in the center of being. Breathe slowly and fully now as you enter that inner point of true power within you.

The **FORCE** of Foundation is non-plused stability. When we apply this, we strengthen our connection to the Victories we seek and need.

The **STATE** of Foundation is ordered, sturdy, relaxed **BEING**. It is the feeling of strength calmly flowing through your limbs and tranquility in your heart of hearts. It is a quiet, clear, alert mind, a keen eye, the gentle yet unshakable inner peace which is fortitude.

Foundation slows down our **FUNCTIONING**. To work on the Foundation of something is to be satisfied with taking care of the details which do not necessarily show, but which serve as the base upon which all that will show must stand. For example, working on the Foundation of a relationship might be improving your attitude toward the other individual, or taking time to consider where you would like that relationship to go. These types of acts represent the inner framework of ordered energies. It is this type of functioning which characterizes the Foundation.

Finally, the tenth Sphere, named The Kingdom, is the Sphere representing completion and the physical or material manifestation of all the work that has gone before. Feel the sense of the completion of any given goal or job, and you enter the Kingdom. Stay there long enough, and the inner Kingdom is manifested on the screen we label "physical" awareness.

The **FORCE** of The Kingdom is its directive influence over the patterning we engage in. By living in its consciousness, we subtly direct the patterns of our fulfillment into the manifest plane. The inner experience of abundance, for example, manifests into arrival on the "external" plane through the agency of our will directing it to that end.

The **STATE** of The Kingdom is the feeling-consciousness-experience of the final phase or results of our operations relative to a given goal.

The **FUNCTIONING** of The Kingdom is efforts directed toward bringing a process to its "earth-plane" conclusion.

We see then that Inner Freedom means the use and application of our own state of being, direction of our feelings, thoughts, and activities at will. Qabala has shown us ten different ways to work with our Inner Selves to gain more and more of that freedom. At the same time it promises that the Inner controls the Outer.

For ages we have been trying to find happiness by controlling external situations. Qabala teaches that those situations are the reflection of our inner state. The more unhappy we become, the more our outer situations will reflect our inner lack and woe. The more dependent we become on the outer, the less the outer will provide of any real meaning.

Inner Freedom means directing our state of consciousness, our forces, and our functioning. The Inner Freedom to experience, express, and manifest is the determining factor of our lives. Qabala gives us that promise, and the way to test it out.

THE QABALIST'S FORMULA FOR FULFILLMENT

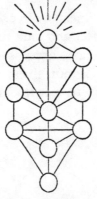

One legend asserts that God gave man Qabala as an alternative to madness. This was probably based on the fact that the Tree of Life offers us a reliable, systematic approach to the handling of any problem, the achieving of any objective. Qabala presents us with an alternative response pattern to fear, panic, blind belief, and stress-filled hope. The ten Spheres on the Tree represent ten things to do for bringing about desired results in a balanced, harmonious way.

As we practice applying this system to our daily works, in time it becomes easier and more automatic to do. The energy we used to waste in stress, fear, and frustration is gradually diverted into more useful, enlightening patterns of calm, effective living.

All our stresses and pains are the product of the pattern our forces flow in. Withdraw our force from those painful patterns, and the pain is without the power to be.

Our joy, peace, love, and enlightenment also require force, travelling in particular patterns, to be. Withdrawing our forces from negative patterns or conditions, we then have that power to direct into more positive states of consciousness and function.

This is the principle value of the Qabala Tree of Life from a practical, daily living standpoint. It shows us what to do with our selves; a way to deal with things that *works!*

Now let us examine how to apply the Tree of life *system* as a whole to particular areas of need. This will serve as a fundamental ground-plan of a ten-part formula for success and fulfillment.

THE FORMULA FOR FULFILLMENT

Bring to mind a particular situation or set of circumstances in your life that is of special importance to you at this time. It may be a personal relationship, a sudden crisis, a financial matter, or something pertaining to your spiritual development. Simply bring to mind one specific problem or concern that you want or feel you need to work on, handle, direct, or control.

Sphere 1: The Crown:

With that concern in mind, begin to apply The Crown. Have a pencil and blank paper handy. To apply The Crown is simply to direct awareness into the situation. Simply keep the area of concern in your consciousness for a time. As you do, make a list of the factors which make it up that you become aware of.

During this process, avoid nervousness or emotionalism. Remain as calm, neutral, and detached as possible. Simply remain conscious of the situation you must handle. Gradually, in time, specific, relevant factors pertaining to it will unfold in your conscious mind through this procedure.

Sphere 2: Wisdom:

To apply Wisdom to the situation or problem direct the focus of your attention to yourself. Carefully observe what you are doing, feeling, thinking, aware of in the **NOW**. Observe how your actions and reactions are affecting you in the **NOW**.Direct your attention to your desires to see what you are wanting. Gradually begin to align your actions and reactions with the bringing about of what you want. Here again it is often helpful to write down your observations and discoveries as they occur.

Sphere 3: Understanding:

With the situation in mind, relax and feel yourself calmly, harmoniously receptive to clearly perceiving what is going on in the situation and what you can do to bring about what you want. Whereas Wisdom is to **DO** that which helps, Understanding is to become aware of, to realize, that which is helpful to do. The former is active doing, the later is receptive perceiving, sensing, knowing.

Relative to this procedure, it is extremely important to watch your mood. Going into the receptive mode can fill us with all the negative emotion and unconstructive thinking we go to Qabala to avoid. Truly useful and good Understanding can only enter and unravel in a balanced, undisturbed, tranquil state.

Entering the receptive, perceptive mode in balance will gradually reflect the coordinates of the situation upon your mind with the clarity of useful Understanding, or at least make clear what to do to acquire the additional data needed.

Sphere 4: Mercy:

Mercy is the application of measured gentleness and

laxity to our process. With the situation of your concern in mind, measure the degree of ease and gentleness with which you are approaching it. Adjust your state until you are radiating sufficient kindness into yourself and your approach. Eliminate all useless tension, excessive stress and emotional strain, while, at the same time, you remain focused on your particular objective. Being Wise, doing that which is helpful, maintain the gentle peace of balanced, harmonious Mercy.

The application of Mercy keeps order and harmony, and therefore attracts more order and harmony to us. To work on a goal or objective outside of Mercy's balance is to be attracting more stress and confusion, thereby actually *repelling* the very peace and happiness we are working so hard to attain.

Sphere 5: Severity:

Severity is the opposite of Mercy and needs to be applied to keep us balanced. Here is where we do that which is necessary to accomplish the task, solve the problem, protect what is important. With what you want to work on in mind, feel yourself at one with the state of competence and self-control. Feel the stern strength and ability to do what must be done, and begin doing it in a balanced, conscious manner.

Sphere 6: Beauty:

With the situation you must handle in mind, direct attention to the Beauty you want to manifest or experience and share through it. Beauty is that transcendent joy we feel in a rapturous moment of music, art, and love. It is a special sensation within, all its own. As we work on consciously contacting it within us, at will, we familiarize with Beauty and find it easier and easier to recall, enjoy, and aim at.

Working on Beauty relative to a goal instantly detaches us from all the lower drives which have been pushing us to near excess. We at once work on the inner, spiritual, energy level and join the ranks of the Heaven Born to all the Universe's delight. Beauty keeps us sane, and human, and working in its influence is the secret of happy, worthwhile work **AND** success.

To work on Beauty means, to some extent, slowing down to work on some of the finer, inner details of your task. Only then can we maintain our conscious union with the subtle vibrations which are Beauty's inner guidance.

Sphere 7: Victory:

To work on Victory simply means keeping before the conscious mind the ultimate sense of what we are striving to **ACHIEVE**. It is keeping the sense of winning, of fulfillment, of complete joy and satisfaction in a job well done. With what you want to achieve in mind, work awareness into the state of your Victory in that area. Keep on guard to notice and instantly eliminate even the *slightest* feeling of defeatism.

Working on Victory requires a calm, relaxed state. Only then can the real inner feelings of achievement and accomplishment sink deep into the core of our being. There in the core, when Victory is made conscious, the rest of our being changes, and the way to win, to surmount, and to arrive will gradually unfold. We achieve all Victories in an expanding spiral pattern. And the spiral begins deep down in our own unconscious depths. In a quiet, peaceful state, inhale fully and gently, feeling the sense of your Victory filling your being with every breath. Gradually, the feeling, sense, and knowing will translate into useful acts of progressive accomplishment in that area. It also begins to attract to us and manifest on its own that on which we are focusing.

Sphere 8: Glory:

To apply Glory to the situation become conscious of your self-worth relative to the task. In other words, begin to feel yourself capable, adequate, good enough to do what must be done. Stay on guard for any trace of the feeling of inadequacy or fear, and instantly replace those with the self-motivated state of your sense of competence.

True Glory begins with real, non-boastful confidence in your **SELF**. As you practice feeling that relative to your goal or objective, your ability to feel and **BE** that way strengthens, deepens, and develops. This actually opens us up to our higher, divine potential which *"can do all things"*.

With the goal in mind relative to a given situation, stay conscious in that light of Glory, that force field or feel of True inner worth. Thus, greater strength and ability flow forth.

Self-worth is never something to try to prove to another. Nor are we to hide behind feelings of superiority and false confidence in a blind refusal to face faults or weaknesses. Rather, look for, accept, and work on the inadequacies of your conduct without feeling you are inferior to the task. Glory is the feeling-sense that you **CAN** change, create better, and grow because limitless potential is yours. In fact, limitless potential is the very nature of your True Self.

Sphere 9: Foundation:

The Foundation of anything is its inner structure relative to its outer manifestation. Foundation is a relative concept in that there is always a deeper, more hidden structure upon which something is based.

To find the Foundation of a given situation or set of coordinates, determine the various parts which, when combined, give birth to or make up the whole.

One helpful exercise is to practice seeing into the Foundation of various manifestations. For instance, look back at the experiences and preparation which ultimately resulted in your present skills and accomplishments. Consider any common household object, and trace it back to its source. For example, a wooden desk had to be found, selected, purchased, shipped. Without those prior steps, or some form of previous activities and preparation, it would not be here. We can also trace the desk's constructive foundation. To be what it is today it had to be lacquered, stained, built. The wood had to be measured, cut, sanded. Then we can trace the desk's Foundation in the preparation, education, and experiences that went into the development of the craftsman who built it.

Another helpful exercise is to practice looking back at the events of our lives, determining what we did to enable what occurred to happen just as it did.

All executions require a stable base of adequate preparation. All our failures and frustrations can be traced back to a lack of preparation, readiness, or ripeness. To work on the Foundation level of your objective is to work on the various skills, strengths, resources, and circumstances required for bringing about what you want in the best possible way. It means to initiate and maintain a momentum of effort aimed in the direction you want events to flow in.

All adequate work begins with a peaceful, ordered, stable state. It is our state of being which, in a very significant sense, is the Foundation of our destiny. A calm and relaxed, centered state of being attracts ordered and harmonious circumstances.

The basic formula for Foundation work upon your objective can be boiled down to four key areas to direct your attention to: *patience, persistence, preparation, and peace.* Just by directing attention to these, and working on that level, begins to generate a deep inner order into the situation which will unfold in peace and success.

Continuing to direct effort and attention on the Foundation level gradually reveals more that we can do for the growth, strength and stability of our objective.

It is important to remember that one can never be perfectly prepared for or in anything. But, when we have done enough, and times are ripe, we find ourselves able to make the breakthrough we have been working for. Then, like a plant that has been busy working and growing underneath the soil, we emerge into the light of a new opportunity.

Sphere 10: The Kingdom:

This is working on the final, apparent outcome of the situation you are dealing with. With the situation in mind, practice seeing, visualizing, feeling and fully experiencing the desired outcome on the physical level. See the smiling faces, the colors and lights. Hear the voices, smell the smells, feel the senses of touch and taste all connected with the final stage of your operation.

To work on the kingdom level means to feel the joy and peace of your fulfillment in that area as well.

The purpose of this inner visioning and experiencing is two-fold. First of all, what we become conscious of begins to manifest in our lives. Secondly, this consciousness soon reveals the particular details we can or need to work on. When we see and experience the finished scene, we discover the areas needing development and work, as well as the aim and direction of our efforts.

In time, through this process, we not only gain a clearer and clearer knowledge of what we want, but also how to get there. Following that map, our manifestation is virtually guaranteed.

* * *

We have seen here a ten part formula for bringing about what we want. Apply it when you become aware of a health need, a desire to move to a new town, or reach a higher level of consciousness. Apply it to every particular need or desire as it arises, and to life as a whole when it all seems so complex and mixed up you are not sure of any particular area to work on.

Our lives are becoming more complex almost daily. Using the above formula, we can sort things out when they seem to be getting out of hand.

In your application of the formula, use your own discretion for the amount of time spent on any or all of the phases. Realize simply that even one moment of application sets into motion a force of order and light. The more time spent on any phase, the more substantial and powerful the results.

During each phase of application, keeping a pencil and paper at hand, write down your observations and discoveries. This makes it easier to notice what is happening, and to realize what to do about it.

All creative processes unfold gradually, first on subtle levels. We may discover something as subtle as changing a feeling to help us discover what to do next or what else we can do for ourselves. The important thing is to do whatever little we can, for this always leads to greater freedom and power.

The more we work with these forces, states, and ways of functioning represented on the Qabala Tree of Life, the more wonderful that Wisdom Teaching becomes. We have to wonder where it comes from, because it works so well, so profoundly well. It provides us with the secret of happiness, the way to live, a way that works.

It is amazing that it could have been around for ages, and we who are just finding out about it are just finding out about it now.

There must be something very special about this time for us.

In any event, at last we have — if not **THE** key — one that is most important. May you use it to open the golden door of your most blessed destiny.

MEDITATING WITH QABALA

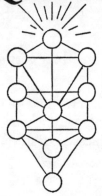

We come now to the final application of Qabala to be covered in this book. This is meditation. By meditating in the forces represented on the Qabala Tree of Life, we become more attuned to them *and* ourselves. At the same time, we generate a force field of peace, order and harmony into our lives.

Meditation offers us the opportunity to experience the highest levels of contentment, clarity, and control. When done and practiced properly, meditation provides healing of ourselves and our life-situations. Through Meditation we can touch the highest Peace Profound and ultimately dwell in the Divine Nature of our True Self. In mundane terms, meditation can be a priceless source of peace and order in our lives.

What is to be described in this chapter is not intended to be regarded as the only form of meditation. It is, however, the form or technique recommended by this author as the safest and most effective he has found to date. Safety is an important factor whenever we work with our consciousness or directly upon our minds. The particular method of meditation which follows is evaluated as safe because the meditator remains and works on improving his or her own conscious self-control throughout the procedure. It is **NOT** recommended by this author to in any way allow the attention to drift, to lose conscious awareness of exactly what you are feeling, "picking up", and radiating in the **NOW** at any time during the practice of **ANY** form of meditation. If the individual does not maintain conscious control of his or her own state of balance, whatever the activity, that balance will not be maintained. As far as this author is concerned, that is as good as Cosmic Law.

One of the primary purposes of the Qabala Tree of Life is to set before us a scheme of self-control. Each Sphere on the Tree represents a state of consciousness, what to be aware of, and how to direct our forces from within. As long as we are anchored or consciously working in one or more of these, we are living and working in a healthy, constructive way. This is not to imply that there are not other healthy, constructive ways to live and work not included in the Tree. However, the Tree offers ten safe and effective Spheres of conscious function. The application of each of the forces it represents will have positive, harmonizing effects at what-ever moment and in whatever situation it is applied.

To meditate means to pay special attention; that is, to so situate ourselves that our level of attention or conscious awareness is at maximum.

We achieve this higher level of awareness first and foremost in stillness. Stillness means not moving. Relative to meditation, stillness is to be applied to the body, emotions, mind, and environment.

The first stage of meditation is to seat yourself comfortably in a quiet room, preferably alone. Any movements by others in the room will diminish the clarity and depth of your attention to some degree.

Sit with spine erect but relaxed. It may help to cross your legs "indian style", but meditation can be just as effective with your feet on the ground and your hands resting on your knees. Follow your own inner feelings in this. Also, during meditation, there is nothing wrong with adjusting your position as needed, as long as it does not increase restlessness or agitation.

The next step is to adjust your breathing. Make your breaths soft, full, and rhythmic. Make sure the lungs are filled to capacity on inhalations, and thoroughly empty on exhalations. This long, rhythmic breathing helps us relax, deepening our stillness. It also stirs up our inner psychic forces. These inner psychic forces are our deeper, hidden drives, feelings, and motivations. The breathing stirs these up, enabling us to become more self conscious, aware on deeper levels of our being.

After some of this conscious, intentional breathing, begin to bring your body into the relaxed state. Look for and eliminate any useless physical tensions.

Next, direct attention to the top of your head. Become aware of the point atop your skull right in the center of the crown of your head. Feel that point with your awareness. Imagine a walnut sized sphere of incredibly brilliant force and light right there.

The ancients taught that right above our head is a center of force. This is only one of seven major force centers located in various places of our force field and connected with our physical body. One is around the genital area. When this force field is activated, we experience it as sexual stimulation and attachment to "things".

Above that is a force center around our solar plexus area. This is the center of our emotional drives, desires, and aggressive tendencies. Sometimes its activation can be felt around the naval area, but its most aggressive activations are felt in our solar plexus.

The next above the solar force center is the heart

center. This is located right around the center of our chest and is the source or channel through which we experience love, harmony, compassion, Beauty.

Above the heart center is the throat center. This is a sphere of force located right around where the male's adam's apple would be. This is the center of sensitive, intuitive awareness.

The next force center going up is located right in the middle of the forehead, just above the eyebrows. This has been called "The Third Eye", and is the center of penetrating Perceptive Insight.

The sixth force center is behind us. It is located at the small of the back, at or around the coccyx, and is called the Sacral Center. This center is the negative pole of the seventh force center, the one located at the crown of the head. Before the Crown Center is fully activated, the Sacral Center awakens, and force passes up and down along our spine along what is called the Sacral Conarial Axis. It is not necessary, for our present purposes, to thoroughly explain what is meant by the full awakening of the Crown Center. At this point, all we need to know about it is that when we have fully mastered our forces, and can keep them conscious and constructive, harmonious and balanced at all times, a new and much greater creative force is released in the being. This force, called "the awakened Kundalini" by the ancients, fully opens the Crown Center and traverses the Sacral Conarial Axis.

The Crown Center is the place of union with our True or Divine Self. When we keep attention here, that is where our forces flow, connecting our consciousness with the deepest and highest part of our nature.

Wherever we direct attention in life, that is where our forces tend to go. By directing attention to the Crown Center, that is where our forces go. If we are not focusing on a given center, our forces tend to go much more "willy nilly" than if that focus of attention is maintained. To direct attention to a given force center simply means becoming aware of that general location on the body, but remembering that the actual force center is part of a more subtle energy body than the physiological organism.

Returning now to our description of meditation relative to the Qabala, direct attention to the force center at the top of the head, and continue your long, quiet breathing. Throughout the process, stay aware of every feeling, every sense happening in or to you in the NOW. And continue to dwell in ever deeper peace and relaxation.

At this point, we are ready to go to work on the Tree. Begin with the first Sphere, The Crown, and meditate on or in the state it represents. Spend about one minute there, and then move on to the state or force field represented by the second Sphere, Wisdom. Continue this process, spending about one minute in each state, descending the Tree in order of the Spheres. When you have completed your work in The Kingdom, then work your way back up to The Crown. The descending order is the first Sphere through the tenth. Then, the reverse or ascending order is the tenth Sphere through the first.

In this meditation procedure, we are just to dwell consciously in the state, forces, and inner functions represented by each Sphere on the Qabala Tree of Life respectively. You can spend as little as ten seconds on each, or as much time as you want. A minimum of thirty seconds is usually required to *settle-in* to the force field. As long as your movement is balanced and settled, calming and conscious, move at the pace you choose.

Let us go through one brief meditation process together. At this point in your reading of the present book, that which the Spheres represent should be easily recalled with merely a key phrase or two. It is recommended that the reader re-read this book gently but frequently until a clear inner sense and familiarity with the forces is established in consciousness.

Also, remember that we are not *thinking* about the forces represented by the Spheres in this meditation. We are to be consciously dwelling in the forces. That is, do not simply mentally reiterate intellectual descriptions of the states, but feel the forces, enter the state described or represented by them. In time, through practice and effort, this becomes easier to do, and our experience of the states much deeper.

Now, to begin. Seat yourself comfortably, and begin to breathe fully and rhythmically. Relax the body and feel deep inner peace flowing through you.

After a few moments of that, direct attention to the force center atop your head, that walnut-sized sphere of brilliant light right in the center of the top of your head. Keep attention there while you continue your rhythmic breathing and relaxation. At the same time, stay as completely conscious as you can of every feeling, vibration, and sense happening to you in the now.

It is not necessary to stop your reading of these instructions during this exercise. While the reading will diminish the depth and clarity of the meditation experience to some degree, at the early phases keeping the instructions with you and reading them as you go can actually serve as more of a help than a hindrance. Our clarity, focus, and self-control progress slowly through practice in meditation. In the early phases, sometimes lasting months or even years, the mind tends to wander, strong restless feeling emerge, and a general tendency toward distraction all serve to obfuscate awareness. Practice and the effort aimed at self-discipline in these areas will gradually make for improvement.

Now, relaxed, breathing rhythmically, with attention

on the force center atop the crown of the head, observing every feeling and sensation and activity happening in you or to you in the now, enter the state represented by The Crown on the Tree of Life. Feel the sense of union with your True or Divine Self and clear perceptive awareness of the True Nature of what is happening.

After thirty seconds or so, enter the second Sphere, Wisdom. Feel your state and forces perfectly aligned with bringing about your True Will or Divine Fulfillment. Dwell in this state.

Next, enter the state represented by the third Sphere, Understanding. Feel perfect insight into what is happening and how it all works unfolding in the depths of your being.

From Understanding, move to Mercy. Feel the balanced gentleness, ease, and peace Mercy represents flowing through your consciousness. Dwell in the forces of Mercy consciously for awhile.

The fifth Sphere, Severity, is next. Here feel and dwell in the sense of justice, discipline, and the strength of will flowing through you. Keep it balanced with gentleness as you allow the forces of Severity to sink deep into the very core and essence of your being in the **NOW**.

The sixth Sphere is Beauty. Enter that now. With attention still fixed at the crown of your head, gently and fully breathing and relaxed, tune into Beauty's electric vibrations within. Sense, feel, and dwell in the conscious awareness of that harmonizing, titillating state of inspiration. Remember that Beauty is that inner feeling-experience triggered off by your favorite melody, vision, or experience of a dream come true. Keep it calm and relaxed, allowing it to flow deep into your consciousness.

Victory is the next state to enter. Dwell in the feelings of triumph, accomplishment, fulfillment of your highest aspirations.

Glory follows. Dwell in the feeling-being sense of your self-worth and virtually limitless capacity to achieve and excel. Allow these feelings of your competence and potential of limitless height in every area to flow through you without emotionalism, egotism, feelings of superiority or antagonism. Stay calm, balanced, and deeply ordered and your feelings of self-worth can penetrate the depths of your being, igniting the spark of heightened creative potential within.

The next state to enter is Foundation. Feel yourself at the inner Foundation level of the universe and self. Sense peace and order flowing through the deeper inner source level of your being, and feel at one with the deeper inner source level of the universe, filling all space with the peace and order in you. With that inner peace and order feel strength and stability as well.

Finally, we arrive at The Kingdom. Here, meditate in the sense and flow of physical manifestation. Simply remain conscious of that feeling and sense of the final, completion phases of operations and the level of earthly or worldly manifestation. Do this as you maintain your perfect peace, breathing rhythmically, with attention at the crown center, observing all that is happening to you and in you in the here-now.

After dwelling in The Kingdom for a time, move back up to the Foundation Sphere. Once again enter the state of inner structural awareness relative to the manifest level. Feel at one with the forces at work "underneath and inside" what **IS**, feeling order, strength, stability, patience, and preparedness as you do.

From the ninth Sphere to the eighth, and we are back at Glory. Once again dwell in your feelings and sense of self-worth, competence, and limitless capability.

From Glory, move back to Victory. Here again dwell in triumph. Not emotionally excited, tense or anxious triumph, but a cool calm knowing and sensing of ultimate fulfillment, attainment and accomplishment.

Now we return to Beauty. Sense that inner state of harmony and rapture you feel when looking at or experiencing that which is Beautiful to you.

Severity is next going up the Tree. Place yourself in the state of the cool, calm strength required for doing what needs to be done, undeterred by pleasure or timidity.

Next dwell once again in Mercy. Here we take it easy. Feel the force of ease and gentleness in you and the universe as a whole.

Understanding comes next. Feel yourself comprehending all the mystery of the universe with perfect lucidity in your consciousness.

From the Knowing characterized by Understanding, we enter the Doing characterized by Wisdom. Enter the state represented by this Sphere once again. Feel yourself entirely aligned with the bringing about of all that is perfectly good in your life. Feel, sense, know, be aware of your forces all perfectly cooperating with your highest wants and truest, deepest needs.

And at last we return to where we started, the first Sphere, The Crown. Here, once more dwell in the consciousness of feeling Divine Union with your True or Highest Self. Feel penetrating perception into the True Nature of what IS in perfect clarity dawning in your consciousness.

That completes our meditation with the Tree. Gently begin to stir, moving your body, perhaps stretching and yawning. Leave the meditation state slowly, maintaining the high feeling and refined awareness thus gained as long as you can.

What we have described is a still form of meditation. There is also a moving form. Moving meditation with the Qabala Tree of Life is done exactly as the still form is except for two changes. One is that we do it during physical movements, exercise, and/or the course of daily living circumstances. The other is that sufficient attention is to be directed to the safe and adequate handling of whatever activities we are involved with at the time.

It is recommended that one practice the still form of the meditation at least twice a day, once in the morning before starting out, and once in the evening before retiring for the night. In conjunction with this, practice the moving form during all exercise and daily living activities. During daily living activity it is not crucial to remember the Sphere you worked on last, or to apply them in perfect sequence. Simply working on them in a more or less balanced manner is enough.

The results of this meditational practice can be tremendously far reaching. In time, our entire personality is transformed, refined, purified. It is purified of the negative, useless tendencies and reaction-patterns. Gradually we become more balanced, ordered, and effective. Our highest and best is brought out, as our limitless potential is freed. All this is then reflected back to us in the pattern of our life situations, our destiny. Our life experiences raise with our own ascension in being and doing. Our relationships, achievements, health, living conditions all reflect our growing power, skills, peace, and joyous abundance.

Keeping our consciousness in the forces and functioning of the Spheres of the Tree works on our subconscious, keeping us oriented to and working upon manifesting the highest possibilities. In time, we are reborn into the image of this new and positive, yet balanced Self. For the subconscious reproduces in line with the data-suggestions it is given.

What we think, feel, and direct our effort and attention to is where our lives will tend to go.

QABALA MEDITATION

Holy Qabala
Tree of Life
Ancient Way
To a whole new life.

There are Ten related Stations
On the sacred Tree
Ten powers to transform ourselves
And Know Eternity.

Awaken to the Process
Take charge of your own life.
The Tree describes a Gnosis,
Arouses Peace in strife.

Sacred, hidden Forces
Blooming on the Cosmic Tree
Here to guide, empower courses
To Divine Reality.

The Crown is Light, Noetic Bright,
It's not the kind most see.
Its Brilliance is Perceptive Sight
Ignited by the Quest To See.

Wisdom is not knowledge
But how to learn and Be
To make the desired happen
By directing our forces Innerly Free.

Understanding slowly unfolds
The Way to Be and How to Go.
It dawns in Conscious Function's Glow
And looking till we calmly Know.

Mercy is the freedom
To live in joy and ease.
It's patience and contentment
For Harmony, Abundance, and Peace.

Severity is doing
In ordered, sequenced steps.
We start at the beginning
And end when the sought is in our nets.

Beauty is our dream
Our grace in the Now and Then.
It is dancing when we move.
It is singing when we speak. Ascend!

Victory is achievement
Triumphing over the odds.
Focusing on our conquest
Failure's bleak charade we dodge.

Glory is respect
Our own and others' too;
Acknowledging our deepest needs
It's our's when we feel fulfilled.

Foundation is our peace and strength,
Endurance and stability.
Maintain self-control when pressed -
Not pushing or yielding - steady be.

The Kingdom is the manifest.
We can manifest what we choose.
Steady work upon this phase
Results in completion - these are Cosmic Rules.

These are the Ten Forgotten Stations,
Power Supplies of the Sacred Tree.
Through these Build a safer nation,
A world, a Man, an Age that's **Free**.

So mote it be

Amen

finis

Also
by Bob Lancer

MASTER YOURSELF MASTER YOUR LIFE

A Practical Guide to
Enlightenment and Success
In Conscious, Creative Harmony
With Natural Laws and Order

A Quality Paperback Book . . . Retail Price $5.95

TRIUMPHANT RELATIONSHIPS

How To Handle Relationships
With Those Who Direct Negativity At Us
And How To Avoid Doing That To Others

A Beautiful Booklet . . . Retail Price $2.95

For further information:
Regarding additional literature and tape cassettes
by Bob Lancer, mail your request to:

BOB LANCER
c/o Limitless Light Publishing
8115-1 N. 35th Avenue
Phoenix, AZ 85051

Bob Lancer is also available for public speaking
engagements.